KU-610-808

HEAT
DUST
and
dreams

For our families, who believed in us.

For the people of the Kunene Region,

who are the guardians of a precious

place. For Carina, who twinkled.

And for my father, Johnny Rice.

'... and the desert shall rejoice and blossom as the rose.'

Isaiah, chapter 35 verse 1

HEAT
DUST

and

dreams

An exploration of people and environment

in Namibia's Kaokoland and Damaraland

Mary Rice *and* Craig Gibson

PREFACE

If there is a recurrent theme in this book, it is undoubtedly change. The winds of change for this once-remote backwater come courtesy of an independent Namibia, with new regional boundaries and a burgeoning tourism industry. The gradual assimilation of the Kunene Region into the national socio-political sphere has very real social and environmental implications. Fragile soils are trampled under the burden of an exploding livestock population whose numbers exceed the capacity of the land to sustain them, while the inhabitants, particularly the Himba, make subtle cultural adjustments as they digest the offerings of the 21st century.

This is especially tangible on the dusty streets of the Kunene Region's capital Opuwo, where progress, with its attendant conveniences and pitfalls, is very much in evidence. It has the atmosphere of a frontier town where people from a medley of cultures rub shoulders – suited government officials and elegant Herero and Himba women in traditional attire move surreally amongst a chaotic flow of battered Ford and Chevrolet pick-up trucks. A *Pep* clothing store sits incongruously on the town's main thoroughfare, the ultimate symbol of the

accession of a cash culture. Opuwo is also distinguished by a profusion of bottle stores that appear to enjoy considerable patronage, judging by the debris that litters the southern approach to the town. A large gathering seated under acacia shade near the centre of town is not a tribal council, but the outlet for a locally brewed alcohol where patrons are served all day, everyday. Nor is this scene confined to the urban sphere. The settlement of Etanga, some hundred kilometres west of Opuwo, has a trading store with a similar clientele. The lure of bottled beer and noxious spirits induces livestock owners to trade a beast for a few quarts – a transaction that is all too often repeated, with ever-diminishing returns for the drinker. Alcoholism is, perhaps, a controversial symptom to highlight, but it is a painfully real, and perhaps inevitable, consequence of the new meeting the old.

We were drawn to north-western Namibia, like many others before us, by its impressive credentials as a wilderness with unique cultural and environmental attributes. European explorers penetrated the region relatively late in the 19th century. All were confronted by rugged, inhospitable terrain that dictated short forays rather than extended reconnaissance. Aridity, coupled with the relative absence of surface water, also precluded the establishment of commercial agriculture or any other significant development. Contemporary Namibian history has further accentuated the region's isolation, it being off limits during the brutal bush war that ensued in the struggle for independence from South Africa. This relative seclusion effectively came to an end with Namibia's independence in 1990. Since then, large numbers of visitors have been lured north, eager to immerse themselves in the 'last wilderness'. This unfortunate tag has had notable consequences for a region almost entirely comprised of communal land. Visitors here are under little obligation to adhere to any formal ordinance – there are potential campsites under every tree. In an area with only basic infrastructure, characterised by ad hoc trails and erratically maintained roads, an assortment of restless urban adventurers, intent on proving their mettle in the 'bush', have succeeded in creating an unsightly network of vehicle tracks and have harassed the region's wildlife. A major objective of this book, therefore, is to stress the fragility of this wilderness in the face of such unprecedented attention.

Bounded by the cold Atlantic and Skeleton Coast to the west, Kalahari sands to the north and east, and the Namib's sand desert to the south, the region is particularly defined by its geographical setting. The cold ocean/warm interior interface is an integral feature of the region's microclimate. Aridity has produced a notable degree of endemism – organisms restricted to this north-west quarter of Namibia and found nowhere else – particularly amongst the region's reptiles, birds and flora. The violent geological past is visible in the breathtaking scale and scope of the landscape, where the blistering red mountains of the escarpment are soon forgotten as one travels west to be met by the coastal desert and the cool breeze of the Atlantic. In addition, northern Namibia boasts a rich archaeological history with an impressive array of rock art galleries that provide a haunting vision of the shamans' world – significant cultural monuments for visitors and locals alike. Africa's largest mammals – notably elephant, rhino and giraffe – are also found here, occupying atypical habitat and presenting an extraordinary symbiosis of wildlife and environment. Furthermore, the scarcity of natural resources, particularly water, has led to remarkable tolerance between the people and wildlife that inhabit the same tracts of country. In addition, Namibia's conservancies point the way forward for community-based resource utilisation in the sub-region, with members benefitting directly from revenue derived from tourism and safari hunting. This process, instituted in the mid-eighties, has confidently built on the premise that local residents are custodians of the wildlife and should therefore manage these resources for their mutual benefit.

It would be naïve and selfish to expect this long-forgotten corner to remain pristine and untainted by the modern world – that one could somehow protect it from itself. It would also be disingenuous to suggest anything other than that the Kunene Region will, inevitably, change . . .

'Change is inevitable . . . Change is constant.'

Benjamin Disraeli

Sections of this publication were made possible through support provided by the US Agency for Development (USAID) Namibia Mission and the World Wildlife Fund (WWF) under the terms of the Co-operative Agreement No. 690-A-00-99-00227-00. The views expressed in this document are those of the editor or contributors and are not necessarily the views of USAID or WWF. The authors gratefully acknowledge the support and interest of these organizations, and that of Dunlop Tyre Services, the Namibia Nature Foundation and Etendeka Mountain Camp.

Struik Publishers
(a division of New Holland Publishing (South Africa) (Pty) Ltd)
Cornelis Struik House
80 McKenzie Street
Cape Town 8001

First published in 2001

1 2 3 4 5 6 7 8 9 10
website: **www.struik.co.za**

Copyright © in text: Mary Rice and Craig Gibson 2001
Copyright © in photographs: Mary Rice and Craig Gibson 2001,
unless otherwise attributed alongside pictures.
Copyright © in map: Helge Denker
Copyright © in published edition: Struik Publishers 2001

Publishing manager: Pippa Parker
Editor: Helen de Villiers
Designer: Janice Evans
Proofreader: Piera Abbott
Indexer: Mary Lennox

ISBN 1 86872 632 0

Reproduction by Hirt & Carter Cape (Pty) Ltd
Printed and bound by Sing Cheong Printing Company Limited, Hong Kong

All rights reserved. No part of this publication may be reproduced, stored in a retrieval system or transmitted, in any form or by any means, electronic, mechanical, photocopying, recording or otherwise, without the prior written permission of the copyright owner(s) or publishers.

JACKET, FRONT COVER:
Fashioned from cattle horn, these traditional ochre and butterfat containers are a necessary accessory for all Himba women. Women collect the gum of the *omazumba* (*Commiphora multijuga*) to perfume the butterfat and the bark of the *omumbara* (*Commiphora virgata*) to grind into an aromatic powder to mix with the ochre before smearing it on their bodies.

JACKET, BACK COVER, CLOCKWISE, STARTING TOP LEFT:
A bottle tree, *Pachypodium lealii*, is eclipsed by storm clouds with attendant rainbow, Damaraland. ■ Black-backed jackal (*Canis mesomelas*) foraging along the windswept Skeleton Coast. Jackal subsist on a catholic diet largely supplied by the relative bounty of the sea. ■ Hairstyle plays a significant role in identifying age stages of both sexes. Young girls have their hair drawn over their heads in two plaits. Upon reaching the pre-puberty stage, these plaits are undone and re-fashioned into a number of twists over the eyes, reducing vision. After puberty the twists are pulled back into the adult women's style. ■ An inquisitive giraffe amongst scrub mopane, Damaraland. In the absence of large trees, giraffe in this region often have to resort to feeding on dwarf shrubs and trees. ■ A spherical engraving that may depict the location of a waterhole. ■ Young Herero girls wear ordinary western dresses and do not expect to acquire a 'big dress' until after they are married when their husband is expected to bear the cost of the 12 metres of dress material required. Many women prefer western-style clothing to the cumbersome dresses worn by their mothers, although older women are proud of their colourful and elaborate traditional dresses. ■ All ears: a scrub hare (*Lepus saxatilis*), common resident of the region.

TITLE PAGES 2 & 3: The millennium brought exceptional rainfall to much of the Kunene Region. Here a brooding array of clouds offloads its precious cargo, Etendeka Mountain Camp.

PAGE 154: An unlikely mountain-top silhouette. Elephant are not averse to climbing the rocky mountains of the region in search of favoured forbs.

PAGE 155, CLOCKWISE, STARTING TOP LEFT: Purros area with some grass cover. ■ Lichens colour rocks on the windward slope of a rise close to the sea. ■ Potentially fatal thick-tailed scorpion, *Parabuthus villosus*. ■ Cetacean remains (aquatic mammals such as toothed whales, dolphins and porpoises), Skeleton Coast.

PAGE 156, LEFT: Giraffe often traverse arid tracts in search of browse. The Atlantic Ocean's dense cool air is clearly visible this early morning (Western Desert). ■ RIGHT: Wilderness Safaris shows guests the spectacular northern dunefield of the Skeleton Coast National Park.

PAGE 157: A bottle tree, *Pachypodium lealii*, is eclipsed by storm clouds with attendant rainbow, Damaraland.

PAGE 158: *Euphorbia virosa* in bloom, pollinated by a host of crawling and flying insects.

PAGE 160, CLOCKWISE, STARTING TOP LEFT: Shop front – Outjo ■ Residents are fully aware of the value of their elephant as evidenced by various artistic impressions. ■ Shop front – Opuwo ■ Shop front – Sesfontein

Contents

ACKNOWLEDGEMENTS

'Gratitude is the hardest of all emotions to express. There is no word capable of conveying all that one feels. Until we reach a world where thoughts can be expressed in words, "Thank you" will have to do.'

AP Gouthey

The Ministry of Environment and Tourism (MET) endorsed our project, lending credibility to the venture and enabling us to access the right people and the right places. Our sponsors, too, put faith in the concept and we are grateful to The Worldwide Fund For Nature (Namibia), The Namibian Nature Foundation, Dunlop Tyre Services (Namibia) and our original 'champion', Dennis Liebenberg. However, as with all enterprises of this nature, we are deeply indebted to a great number of individuals, many of whom we met as strangers. Without their hospitality and generosity of spirit, we never would have produced this book. First and foremost we must thank Dennis Liebenberg for providing a couple of itinerant gypsies with a home, for providing a welcome refuge from the rigours of bush life and for *always* being pleased to see us. He also contributed generously toward our not inconsiderable fuel bill, a great financial burden for any field project. Malcolm Taylor at Dunlop Tyre Services was another supportive benefactor, whose team replaced our frayed rubber promptly and efficiently whilst he shared his extensive experiences in the bush with us. Pippa Parker and her team at Struik have been enthusiastic and supportive of the concept from an early stage and we applaud them for their encouragement. And finally, we must recognise the undaunted, and unfailing, support of Cynthia and Jim Gibson who were, quite simply, always there. Other individuals and organisations provided a plethora of advice, accommodation, humour, entertainment, guidance and encouragement, all of which enabled us to realise our intended objectives. We do not have the words to thank them enough.

AUTHORS' NOTES

Willie & Cecilia Alberts (Outjo), Monika Uses (Khowarib), Boni Awarab and family (Rooivlak), John Awarab (Palm), Charl & Salome Botes (Kamanjab), Phillida Brooke-Simons (Cape Town), Dr Chris Brown (Windhoek), Japie, Kieks, Debbie, Jaco and Eben Burger (Kamanjab), Richard Coomber (UK), Dr Colin Craig (Windhoek), Barbara Curtis (Windhoek), Anna Davis (Windhoek), Lorna Davis (Swakopmund), Helge Denke (Windhoek), 'The Guys' at Etendeka Mountain Camp (Daniel, Gottlieb, Tensie, Adolf, Elias), Chris Eyre (Namutoni), Julian Fennessy (Windhoek), Vitalus Florry (Bergsig) Petrika Ganases (Khowarib), Yvan Francey (Switzerland), Duncan Gilchrist (Poor Boys Bar), Mike Godfrey (Crazy Kudu, Windhoek), Oom 'Grobbie' Grobler (Swartbooisdrift), Allan Hendry (Okahandja), Joel & Mannetjie Hoeb (Khowarib), Elsie & Rudi Imhoff (Windhoek), Ilvia & Wayne McAdam (Outjo), Dr Margaret Jacobsohn (Wêreldsend), John Kasaona (Sesfontein), Holgar Kolberg (Windhoek), Ruth Kuzatjike (Opuwo), Dr Keith Legget (Windhoek), Blythe Loutit (Swakopmund), Mr Mbango (Windhoek), Ruhara Muhenje (Otjitanda), Colin Nott (Windhoek), Elizabeth Nunes (Brandberg West), Garth Owen-Smith (Wêreldsend), Palmwag Lodge, John and Barbara Patterson (Mowe Bay), Joseph Paulus (Otjinungwa), Pension d'Avignon (Swakopmund), Moira Prior (UK), Kuva Rutari (Onjuva), Stephi Schneider (Windhoek), HO Reuter (Swakopmund), Markus Roman (Spaarwater), The Scientific Society (Windhoek), Rina Sherman (Etanga), Tiens Strandloper (Skeleton Coast), Kozongombe Tjingee and family (Otjitanda), Tjahorerwa Tjisuta (Orupembe), Herman van Wyk (Windhoek), Koos Verwey (Otjinungwa), Chris Weaver (Windhoek), Rensie and Uwe Weimann (Outjo), Chris Greathead, Iain Derrick and Ella Street at Wilderness Safaris (Windhoek), Chris Bakkes and team (Wilderness Safaris, Skeleton Coast Camp).

Clarification is needed on the use of certain terms in this work. Readers should be aware that the Kunene Region is the post-independence designation for a portion of the former districts of Kaokoland and Damaraland. The Kunene Region lies roughly within the boundaries of the Ugab River in the south and the Kunene River in the north. In the east it stretches to the town of Outjo, where a boundary can be traced north around Etosha's western border, passing the new district capital at Opuwo, before arriving at a point just west of Ruacana on the Angolan border. Additionally, the term 'the Kaokoveld' was also used to refer to the combined area of the above-mentioned districts. The three politically defunct names – Kaokoland, Damaraland and Kaokoveld – still enjoy common usage, particularly in the tourism industry. In the text we revert to the colonial terms in their historical context, while using Kunene Region or North-West in all contemporary references.

Our focus on the Himba does not aim to perpetuate ethnic categorisation; rather, the Himba represent an interesting point of reference for examining the resilience of a historically isolated 'traditional' culture. The 'One Nation' ideal that is projected as the model of contemporary nationhood cannot disregard the positive role that significant cultural diversity plays in maintaining the vibrant character of a country. The inclusion of the transcribed personal profiles is intended to give readers a perspective of this diversity through the voices of regular people. The larger mammals also occupy centre stage in this work. This is more a reflection of the nature of this work, which is intended as an environmental documentary and not as a definitive natural history of the region. There is more to the region than charismatic behemoths and glamorous nomads – the desert is home to an unexpected diversity of life, more competently, and appropriately, covered by field guides.

'The State shall actively promote and maintain the welfare of the people . . . policies aimed at . . . maintenance of ecosystems, essential ecological processes and biological diversity of Namibia and utilisation of living natural resources on a sustainable basis for the benefit of Namibians, both present and future . . .'

The Constitution of the Republic of Namibia, Article 95

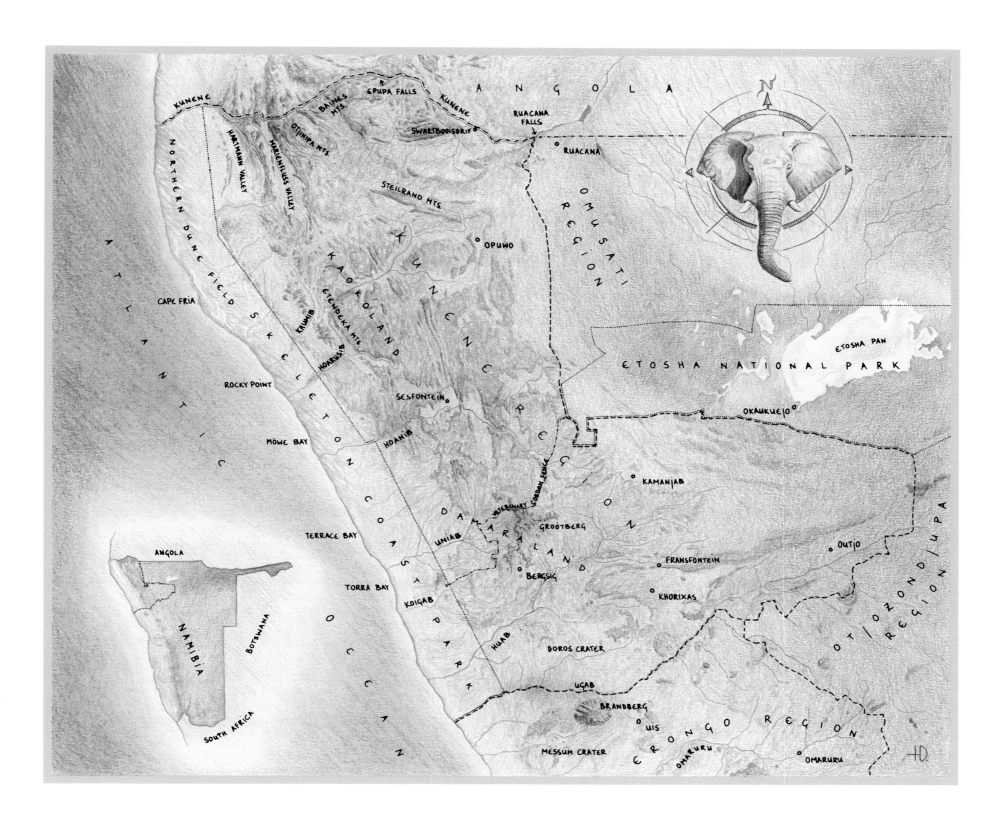

landscape

a geographical window

'There is a pleasure in the pathless woods

There is rapture on the lonely shore

There is society, where none intrudes,

By the deep sea, and music in its roar:

I love not man the less, but nature more.'

Bertrand Russell
Unpopular Essays (1950), 'Philosophy and Politics'

OPPOSITE: *Cyphostemma currorii*, butter trees,
provide the foreground for an expansive vista of
the rugged, eroded Etendeka lava field of Damaraland.

RIGHT: The Hunkab River canyon – cut by the exceptional
rains of 2000. This river has a small catchment in the western
desert and usually ends in the dunes of the Skeleton Coast Park.
These floods saw it reach the ocean, an extremely rare occurrence.

© ORBIMAGE

This image, photographed from the NASA space shuttle above south-western Africa, shows the powerful east wind blowing sand out to sea. The natural features in the region are clearly highlighted: the Etosha Pan (extreme right); the Brandberg Mountain (centre); the Namib Dune Sea (extreme left), and the Etendeka lava field (due west of the Etosha Pan feature).

EVEN THE MOST DISPASSIONATE OBSERVER cannot help but be moved by north-west Namibia's remarkably diverse landscape heritage. This graphic record of geological activity through the millennia has the capacity to distract, threatening to overshadow the people and wildlife that inhabit this distant corner of Africa. Aridity has ensured that these physical features remain unobscured by vegetation or by any significant human development. Indeed, they comprise some of the most striking landmarks in the sub-continent. Expansive horizons are interrupted by a host of distinct features: from the ancient metamorphic rocks that resist the Epupa Falls' persistent flow to the amorphous northern Dune Sea and the primeval sub-volcanic plug that constitutes the Brandberg massif.

The proximity of the South Atlantic high pressure cell, which prevents moisture-laden air from reaching much of western Namibia, and the frigid Benguela current that courses up the south-western coast are the primary agents that dictate the acute aridity of the Namib Desert. These factors inhibit any conventional convection along this confined shore, leaving fog and the inherent humidity of the coast as the primary sources of moisture.

The abundant store of sand found along the Namibian coast, funded by sediment carried to sea by the various rivers, generates a mass of mobile sand dunes as it is blown north by the prevailing south-westerly wind. The desert, particularly its sand dunes, is the region's youngest visible geological feature, commonly thought to have evolved some five million years ago at the onset of the current 'dry' climatic regime. Dunes dominate the southern Namib between Walvis Bay and Lüderitz – the main body of the great 'sand sea'. In the Kunene Region dunes occur intermittently from around Torra Bay and on into southern Angola, comprising the northern dune field.

The adjoining gravel plains, or pro-Namib, are broken by precipitous inselbergs – islands of life with a diverse flora and fauna – that hint at the proximity of the relatively well-watered escarpment to the east. This diversity intensifies along the escarpment zone that separates the savanna of the eastern hinterland from the coastal desert, where a profusion of endemic plant and animal species reflects the multiplicity of biological niches.

ETENDEKA LAVA FIELD

The expansive, rugged Etendeka lava field that straddles the escarpment and the gravel plains of the pro-Namib epitomises the aura of the region. Reminiscent of a vegetated Martian surface, it evidences an unstable period of volcanic activity some 130 million years ago. Up to a kilometre thick in places, these basalts were formed by solidified magma that flowed out of large-scale fissures in the earth's surface. This activity marked the onset of the impending fragmentation of Gondwanaland – the southern super-continent comprised of Antarctica, Africa, India, South America and Australia. These lava flows have further strengthened the theory of plate tectonics, having been matched to similar rocks on Brazil's distant shore.

The Etendeka lava field is large enough to be discernible in remote images captured by orbiting spacecraft. Erosion has sculpted this landscape into a variety of features including flat-topped mesas, precipitous buttes and a myriad braided washes. Further north, glacial action is evident in the upper Hoarusib River's catchment, where the sculpted valley floors attest to the passage of these frozen rivers some 200 million years ago.

FAIRY CIRCLES – *Fact or fancy?*

NORTH-WEST NAMIBIA'S OTHERWORLDLY CHARACTER IS ENHANCED by the scattered occurrence of bare, grass-fringed, spherical depressions that punctuate the pro-Namib's grassed plains from just south of the Orange River to southern Angola. These peculiarities, locally termed 'fairy circles', typically extend from a few metres in diameter, to the larger fifteen-metre examples found in the northern Hartmann's Valley. They resemble a pockmarked lunar surface, revealing the grey or rusty red colour of the soil substrate, and are an intriguing anomaly of the region. Like the human inspired 'crop circles' of the western world, fairy circles have not been conclusively explained.

The most probable theory to date is that postulated by Professor Eugene Moll, formerly of the University of Cape Town, who undertook a comprehensive investigation of this phenomenon. An earlier hypothesis that the soil had been tainted by the toxicity of pre-existing *Euphorbia damarana* shrubs was not borne out by the germination trials he conducted. These demonstrated that the soil within the depressions is, in fact, fertile and capable of sustaining life. A further theory identifies them as hardpans with layers of compacted soil that inhibit water infiltration, rendering the area infertile, whilst a geological suggestion that the rings result from sinkholes in the underlying calcrete substratum has received little authoritative endorsement.

The related mounds known as '*heuweltjies*' that dot South Africa's south-west coast are less enigmatic. In this case, a pair of industrious subterranean residents, namely termites and molerats, are the likely architects of these fertile havens, with both species identified as inhabitants of the mounds. The feeding strategy of individual termite colonies is also a plausible explanation for the even spatial distribution of the *heuweltjies*.

Whilst the fairy circles further north are not fertile havens, all evidence points to prior termite activity at the sites. Professor Moll also analysed the density and chemical composition of the soil inside the fairy circles. This revealed a high clay content that is consistent with termite activity. Furthermore, he attributes the lack of vegetation within the circles to the surface foraging behaviour of termites that typically harvest dry grass from the surface and store it in their underground nests.

An intriguing anomaly of the region . . .

Respected ecologist Ken Tinley, who surveyed the region in the 1970s, speculated that the circles were 'probably fossil termite mounds, now truncated, from a geological period when the region received a higher rainfall'. This theory is given further credence by the fact that harvester termites inhabit spherical subterranean nests of a similar size, up to six metres in depth, whose circumference is dependent on the number of residents. This is, rationally, the most likely, though unproven, explanation for the occurrence of fairy circles. Conclusive proof might have to wait for a period of higher rainfall . . . or the capture of a fairy.

OPPOSITE: *Fairy circles dot the grassed Marienfluss Valley floor, revealing the colour of the soil strata.*

The Hoanib River in flood in its middle reaches. The rivers run red, full of eroded soil from the upstream catchment.

Precipitation cascades off cliffs and hills into erosion gullies that, in turn, converge into rivers.

RIVERS RUN WEST

Namibia is the driest country south of the Sahara, with few perennial rivers between the two that delimit its northern and southern borders: the Kunene and Orange rivers. The Kunene River, which gives its name to the north-west region, originates in the humid Angolan highlands and flows through a dense stand of sub-tropical vegetation for much of its course. This is in stark contrast to the nominally dry 'sand rivers' that erode off the broken rump of the Great Escarpment. These extend from the remote northern Khumib to the expansive Ugab catchment in the south and are a crucial element in the ecology of the area.

Although these, now dry, riverbeds define the contemporary river courses, geomorphological evidence suggests they were once large perennial rivers that drained the interior. They do, however, still flow as unseen subterranean waterways, accumulating precipitation in the more humid eastern escarpment, an essential fund for the relatively arid western reaches that penetrate the pro-Namib.

The erratic rainfall regime here is dependent on moisture inflows from the inter-tropical convergence zone that moves south over this parched expanse during the summer, commonly arriving in angry, moisture-laden storms. Accelerated by altitude, precipitation cascades off cliffs and hills into erosion gullies that, in turn, converge into rivers. These rivers reverberate with the deluge that is commonly the aftermath of these violent thunderstorms, but seldom flow for more than a few hours, and must ultimately break through a wall of sand dunes to reach the sea. Some, like the Hoarusib River with its vast catchment, experience significant floods and regularly reach the Atlantic. Sporadic flooding is crucial in maintaining groundwater resources downstream, a vital reserve that sustains the riverine vegetation as well as numerous springs and wetlands that distinguish the region's rivers. The debris carried by the floods is rich in organic matter, replenishing the soils downstream which, in turn, support the growth in the Hoanib River's broad floodplain, an important wet-season refuge for elephant in particular.

BELOW: The Hoanib River in flood accumulates against rock outcrops and sand dunes before breaking through to the Atlantic Ocean.

RIGHT: The path of the flood from the river's floodplain (the dark mass at extreme right in this aerial photograph) crosses the dunefield, centre, and enters the ocean at left.

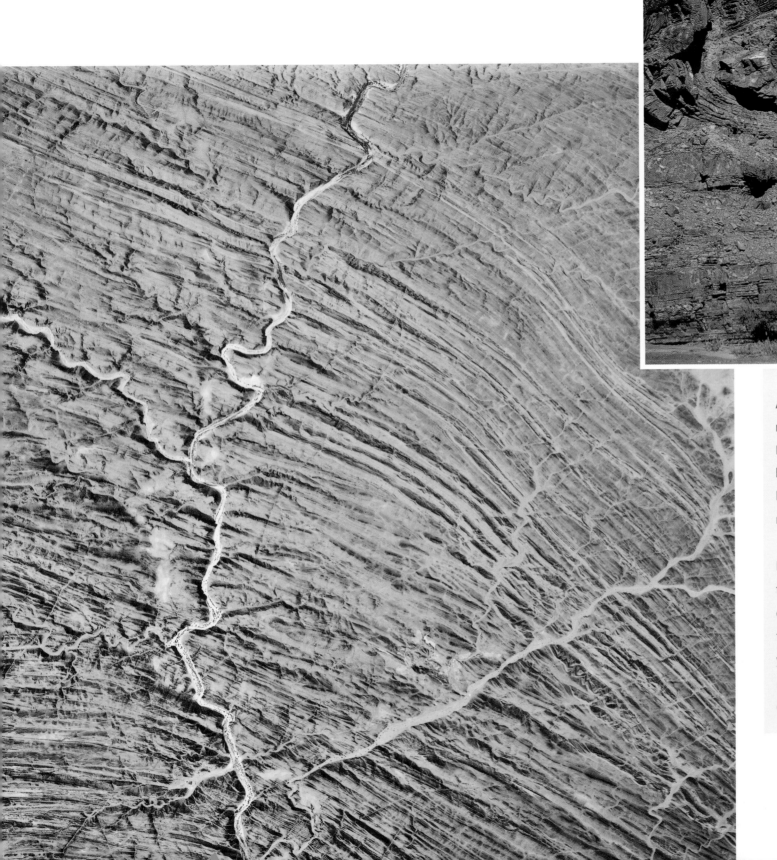

ABOVE: A spectacular vertical face of metamorphic rocks in a tributary of the Ugab River. These contorted schists and quartzites bear silent testimony to the massive geological forces that pushed up Namibia's mountain chains over 500 million years ago.

LEFT: From the air, the rock layers resemble time-etched wood grain. The Ugab River, at centre, has patiently cut its way through these sequences over the past two million years. Large trees, camelthorn (*Acacia erioloba*) and ana (*Faidherbia albida*), are visible as dark spots in the rivercourse.

LEFT: Hoarusib River in the dry season, with some flow from the spring in the riverbed.

BELOW: Hoarusib River in flood; the generous rains that fell across much of southern Africa in 2000 swelled the normally dry riverbed, here at Purros.

ABOVE: Hoarusib River, post-flood, 2000. Sporadic flooding is crucial in maintaining groundwater resources downstream – a vital reserve in sustaining the riverine vegetation that distinguishes the region's rivers. OPPOSITE: *Tribulus zeyheri*, devil thorn carpet, Damaraland, March 2000. *Tribulus* provide a temporary splash of colour in an otherwise monochrome setting.

Springs

Springs are another valuable feature of the region, where water is forced to the surface by impermeable bedrock. They are a crucial element in allowing people, livestock and wildlife to inhabit this otherwise hyper-arid environment. Semi-nomadic Herero and Himba pastoralists rely on such sources to extend their dry season range beyond deteriorating local conditions, particularly if the rains fail. The Kunene's wildlife is equally dependent on these vital springs. At certain times of the day, sandgrouse can be observed flying vast distances to drink, and can congregate in their thousands at these localities. The scattered oases also serve as strategic staging posts for the region's arid-adapted elephant population, enabling them to cross the waterless expanses between their riverine refuges. They are, therefore, a crucial natural spatial regulatory mechanism for people and wildlife.

LEFT: A relatively lush scene — one of many wetlands in the Hoarusib River's course.

OPPOSITE, LEFT: Algae-topped spring, Damaraland. Springs are dependent on rainfall to replenish their subterranean store, and may disappear in an extended dry cycle.

OPPOSITE, RIGHT: Springs are a crucial element of the ecology of the region, particularly in the arid western reaches. They provide sustenance to a host of desert-dwelling wildlife ranging from large mammals such as black rhinoceros (*Diceros bicornis bicornis*) and Hartmann mountain zebra (*Equus zebra hartmannae*) to the region's mobile flocks of sandgrouse (*Pterocles* sp.).

LEFT: Two Palms
Spring, Uniab
River Canyon.
A popular picnic
spot for visitors
and an important
dry-season water
source for the
area's wildlife.

OPPOSITE: A spring
in the desolate
pro-Namib peters
out into the sand.

Sand rivers

The sand rivers that transect this corner of Namibia are remote threads of life. One of these, the northern Khumib River, supports mature stands of mopane (*Colophospermum mopane*) and leadwood (*Combretum imberbe*) trees in its upper reaches, the density of these dwindling as the river enters the Skeleton Coast Park on its journey to the sea. Small numbers of giraffe (*Giraffa camelopardalis*) subsist on the meagre browse available, while a handful of cheetah (*Acinonyx jubatus*) continue to prey on the springbok (*Antidorcas marsupialis*), small mammals and birds resident here.

The middle and upper reaches of the catchment host transitory Himba pastoralists who excavate wells in the dry riverbed to sustain their hardy herds of cattle, goats and sheep. Further south, the Hoarusib River is comparably verdant, with a decidedly Mediterranean character, due in part to the presence of the tamarisk scrub (*Tamarix usneoides*) that forms dense stands on its banks.

Numerous springs also surface here to create wetlands that sustain unexpected residents such as Egyptian geese (*Alopochen aegyptiacus*), as well as the increasingly visible numbers of cattle near the settlement at Purros. The middle reaches of the river are notable for a profusion of palm trees (*Hyphaene petersiana*), the seeds of which originated from the interior, deposited here courtesy of the annual floods.

The Hoanib River is an important refuge for the wildlife of the region and epitomises the dilemma of sustaining tourism in this restricted environment. It is

LEFT: The irregular growth form of certain palms on the Kunene River may be the result of fire damage.

OPPOSITE: This stand of *Hyphaene petersiana*, makalani palm, at the verdant and aptly named spring-oasis of Palm, are out of their recognised range. The region's wandering elephant, being partial to the fibrous fruits, may have imported the seeds in their guts.

the epicentre of elephant viewing and draws a steady stream of organised tours, film crews and casual visitors to the area. In the narrow confines of the river valleys, the increased vehicle traffic has left elephant and other wildlife stressed and traumatised. An indifferent landlord and no formal control on visitor access to this national heritage site have compounded the problem. Furthermore, a multitude of land-use needs must also be catered for in the catchment area. These include livestock farming, agriculture and tourism, as well as the refuge it must provide for wildlife.

The rivers, as linear ecosystems, do not currently benefit from any comprehensive, coordinated land-use plan. A comparatively small fraction of the river systems receive formal conservation protection in the form of the Skeleton Coast Park, the boundaries of which incorporate the lower reaches of the rivers. Upstream activity, however, is the real threat, specifically unsustainable extraction of groundwater that fuels the growth of livestock numbers and extends the scope of agricultural activity.

Damming the rivers would also diminish the effects of the crucial annual floods that are a fundamental element of the ecology of the river systems. All determinants point to a holistic strategy to encourage a sustainable existence that protects resources crucial to man and beast.

The versatile ANA TREE

THE LARGER EPHEMERAL RIVERS are defined by two equally impressive species: the arid-adapted elephant (*Loxodonta africana*) and the versatile ana tree (*Faidherbia albida*). Over four thousand ana trees line the Hoanib River alone, and the ample boughs of these magnificent trees provide shade and shelter for a host of creatures. Ana trees, and particularly their pods, are an indispensable resource for both people and wildlife in the region. The moist, alluvial and sandy soils of the rivers allow the energetic taproots to penetrate the water table and flourish. The trees are unusual in that they come into leaf and drop their pods at the height of the dry season, a time of year when most other trees are dormant and browse resources elsewhere are exhausted. Consequently, a variety of wildlife including elephant, giraffe and gemsbok, as well as domestic livestock, can be found munching fallen pods beneath mature trees.

With a broad continental distribution, reaching as far north as Syria and Israel, the ana tree is renowned for the taxonomic controversy it has caused amongst botanists. Originally classified in the genus *Acacia*, the species has subsequently found a home in its own monotypic genus, *Faidherbia*, where it resides on the basis of a number of distinguishing characteristics, such as its fused stamens. The ana is the most important fodder tree in West Africa's Sahel region, where the reddish-brown pods are traded at market to supplement livestock diets – both pods and leaves have a higher digestible protein content than dry grass. The trees are also encouraged to grow amongst crops, as they enhance the nitrogen content of the soil. Trees in the Kunene Region, among the largest specimens of their kind, produce an estimated 50–150 kg of pods annually, allowing local farmers to collect and store this resource for the leaner dry season.

OPPOSITE: A scarred ana tree (Faidherbia albida) trunk, resulting from the attention of elephant, which are partial to feeding on the bark. ABOVE: An ana tree catches the final rays of a Ugab River evening.

LEFT: An aerial view of the Doros crater complex. Visible as a dark mass (lower left), it is one of several such prominent features in the region, including the more notable Brandberg massif that thrust through ancient folded metamorphic rocks some 135 million years ago.

BELOW: Looking across the southern rim of the boulder-strewn scree slopes of the Doros igneous complex. The exposed granitic boulders typically weather to a rounded shape in the harsh desert environment.

Commiphora, a resilient presence amongst the martian scape of rock and gravel, subsists in the Doros crater.

ABOVE: *Welwitschia mirabilis*, denizen of the Namib, taking advantage of a rare shower of rain that has prompted a temporary flush of grass in a perennially parched wash.

BELOW: Female specimen of *Welwitschia mirabilis*, with aged cones and prominent stem.

A UNIQUE ASSEMBLAGE OF FLORA

An especially diverse botanical heritage, largely determined by variability in rainfall, further distinguishes the region. This ranges from the lush riparian forest of the Kunene River and the arid savanna that dominates the east of the territory to the dwarf shrubs and lichens of the coastal desert. Floral inhabitants also reflect the demands of this austere environment, manifest in various physical traits that sustain their apparent stubborn isolation.

The *Welwitschia mirabilis*, perhaps the most enigmatic floral inhabitant of the continent, epitomises the unique character this arid quarter has imposed on its residents. The plant has a restricted distribution, inhabiting a narrow band of the pro-Namib from the Kuiseb River to southern Angola, favouring dry washes and drainage lines. This distribution largely coincides with the fog belt, although the plants are unable to absorb this moisture directly. *Welwitschia* is essentially a dwarf tree, having evolved a stubby subterranean trunk in response to the advent of an increasingly arid climatic regime. From this submerged base, two broad green leaves sprout and grow for the duration of the plant's life, an anomaly in a region where arid-adapted flora employ succulence or a significant reduction in leaf surface area to limit moisture loss. Part of its secret lies in a reflective cuticle that shields the considerable surface area of the leaves and reduces the impact of the relentless radiation. Soil temperatures beneath the broad foliage have been recorded to be 15°C–30°C lower than the ambient soil temperature, providing a valuable thermal refuge for insects, rodents, reptiles and birds.

On discovery, *Welwitschia*'s exact position in the classification lexicon was ambiguous, providing taxonomists with a genuine dilemma. The plant possesses attributes of 'simple' gymnosperms (plants with 'naked' seeds borne in cones) as well as characteristics of angiosperms (plants that flower and produce fruits). Along with pollen-producing anthers, the numerous smaller, male cones possess a single sterile ovule, thought to evidence a transition to an advanced flowering stage. The female plant possesses fewer, considerably larger, cones that turn an attractive rusty red when mature.

LEFT: The Messum Crater, showing one of a number of near-circular igneous volcanic intrusions, characterised by concentric formations of varying mineral composition. The harder, more resistant outer rocks have weathered to form a rim to the lunar-like 'crater'.

BELOW: *Welwitschia mirabilis* is one of the few floral inhabitants of the area.

OPPOSITE: *Welwitschia mirabilis* on the desolate gravel plains of the pro-Namib.

RIGHT: Welwitschia First Day Cover

(©Nampost. Artist: Helge Denker)

'This is assuredly the most extraordinary plant that exists in intertropical Africa.'

Friedrich Welwitsch (1859)

Welwitschia mirabilis came to the attention of the world with its purported discovery in southern Angola in 1859 by Austrian physician and field naturalist Friedrich Welwitsch. His proclamation: 'This is assuredly the most extraordinary plant that exists in intertropical Africa' set the scene for an intriguing period of claims and counter-claims. The Royal Botanical Garden at Kew was the first institution to receive notification of Welwitsch's discovery of 'a dwarf tree with two opposite leaves, often a fathom long by two to two-and-a-half feet broad, each of them split into numerous ribbon like segments'. However, he did not include a specimen with his description.

A little further south, artist Thomas Baines was actively documenting the natural history of the sub-region, having accompanied a number of notable expeditions as far afield as present-day Zimbabwe. He was very nearly credited with the discovery of the plant after forwarding a specimen from the present-day Swakopmund area, together with sketches, to Kew. They arrived after Welwitsch's Angolan missive, and led to the Austrian receiving the honour of the generic name, conforming to the dictum of taxonomical precedence. *Welwitschia bainesii* persisted in literature until fairly recently but has since been superseded by *mirabilis*, denoting the extraordinary nature of the plant.

It is likely that other Europeans had come across the plant prior to Welwitsch's encounter. An A B Wallaston of the Walvisch Bay Mining Company is recorded as having collected two of the plants in 1857 and forwarding them to the Botanical Gardens in Cape Town, only to have the specimens overlooked by staff. The explorer and author James Chapman is credited with photographing *Welwitschia* in the Swakop River area in 1859. This remarkable feat took the plant, together with other images of Damaraland, to the World Exposition of 1867 in Paris.

The plant's longevity has generated as much interest as has its singular appearance. Carbon-14 dating has determined medium-sized plants to be hundreds of years old, with larger specimens probably significantly older. The plant is further distinguished by playing host to an insect, *Probergrothius sexpunctatis*, which is found exclusively in association with *Welwitschia*. It feeds on ovules of the cone, inadvertently infecting them with a fungus that renders fewer than 2% of thousands of seeds fertile. Enjoying protected status in Namibia and drawing visitors from far afield, the Afrikaans name for the plant, *Tweeblaarkanniedood* ('two-leaf-cannot-die'), is particularly appropriate – testament to the *Welwitschia*'s two most significant attributes.

Other plants in this unforgiving environment have effected a variety of strategies to limit moisture loss, most conspicuous in the array of bloated trees and shrubs that adorn the region. These range from the butter tree (*Cyphostemma currorii*) to elephant's foot (*Adenia pechuelii*) and the sesame bush (*Sesamothamus guerechii*). Swollen stems are particularly conspicuous in *Euphorbia virosa*, a plant similar in appearance to the unrelated cacti family. *E. virosa* has become notorious for the virulent poison of its milky latex, an

The artist Thomas Baines was nearly credited with the discovery of *Welwitschia* after coming across the plant in the present-day Swakopmund area. He produced these remarkable images which were reproduced in the journal of the Linnean Society in 1862. ABOVE: Adult female plant with stem and roots; BELOW: Female cones.

effective defence against the attention of most herbivores – with the exception of the simple, prehistoric stomach of the black rhinoceros. These animals are undeterred by the plant's sharp spines and are recorded as being capable of consuming entire *E. virosa* specimens. An intriguing question, yet one that remains unanswered, is raised by the potential effect of steroids present in the latex of *E. virosa*, on rhinoceros behaviour. In humans, steroids control sexuality and the reproductive activity of males and females. Intriguingly, rhino in the west of Etosha National Park with access to *Euphorbia* are reputedly more fertile than animals in the east, where the plant does not occur.

Euphorbia damarana is physically an altogether different plant with the broad branches found in *E. virosa* replaced by a profusion of thin, rod-like branches. Unlike *E. virosa*, which are invariably perched on precipitous cliffs, *E. damarana* inhabit even-surfaced terrain, commonly occurring together in dense stands on gravel plains where they dominate the scrub component. They also provide unintended shelter for birds like the vivid bokmakierie shrike (*Telophorus zeylonus*), diminutive insectivores such as elephant shrews (*Elephantulus* sp.)

Euphorbia virosa against a backdrop of bleached Stipagrostis grass, Damaraland. The plant's toxic latex makes it an unattractive browse option for most herbivores.

Commiphora is a hardy, arid-adapted species, only coming into leaf after sufficient rainfall.

LEFT: *Cyphostemma currorii*, butter trees, are leafless for most of the year.

BELOW: *Commiphora* sp. Epupa.

BELOW, BOTTOM: *Commiphora kraeuseliana*, an endemic species, seen here north of the Brandberg, where it maintains its leafless vigil for much of the year.

and ground squirrels (*Xerus princeps*). Antelope, too, retreat behind the *E. damarana* to escape the powerful east wind, whilst elephant (*Loxodonta africana*) use them as convenient mattresses, reducing the unfortunate subjects to a compressed mass. Sometimes they do not recover from this experience.

A partiality for rocky terrain makes the *Commiphora* genus particularly at home in the irregular North-West, with five endemic species that range from *Commiphora multijuga*, a smooth, purple-barked tree, to *Commiphora kraeuseliana*, a low-branching shrub. A distinguishing feature of these plants is the aromatic latex that identifies them as members of the frankincense family. They are deciduous, losing their leaves during the dry season – thereby minimising water loss – and will only sprout new growth after sufficient rain has fallen.

memory

a rich archaeological record

'Memories are hunting horns Whose sound dies away in the wind'

Guillaume Apollinaire
1880–1919

RIGHT: Various animal tracks at Twyfelfontein.

OPPOSITE: A spherical engraving that may depict the location of a waterhole.

RIGHT: Vandalism, Twyfelfontein.

BOTTOM RIGHT: Giraffe are a common subject in the engravings of the Kunene Region, here accompanied by ostrich, amongst other species.

OPPOSITE: The 'lion panel', one of thousands of engravings that litter the Twyfelfontein site, an alfresco gallery with expansive vistas over the once game-rich countryside.

FOLLOWING PAGES: Abstract panel, Twyfelfontein. Contemporary scholars look to the San spiritual world in an effort to interpret the images and attribute meaning to them.

The numerous paintings and engravings of the region commemorate another time and mode of existence.

THE LEGACY OF ART

UT WHAT OF THE HUMAN HISTORY of this remote locale? Archaeological evidence indicates that hunter-gatherers spent intermittent periods living in basic structures throughout the Kunene region. The relative bounty of the Atlantic sustained people, the so-called *strandlopers* or beachcombers, along the hostile Skeleton Coast – the stone semi-circular bases of their shelters having been located at resource-rich river mouths and seal colonies. Sites where early settlements occurred in the interior are invariably close to springs or the ephemeral river courses.

The primary legacy of aboriginal peoples is most obvious in the numerous engravings and paintings that commemorate another time and mode of existence. North-western Namibia is particularly well endowed with pre-historic 'rock art'. Paintings and engravings can be found at a variety of locales and depict a diverse array of subject matter. Two prominent sites, at the Brandberg massif and the now-defunct farm Twyfelfontein, are amongst the most significant in the sub-region, with over two thousand engravings at Twyfelfontein alone.

HEAT, DUST *and dreams*

These alfresco galleries are often elevated with expansive vistas over the surrounding countryside and attendant wildlife. It is not difficult to picture the artists clambering up to these open-air galleries, receiving inspiration from the wildlife below them to create their masterpieces. The arid-adapted fauna of the region and geometric patterns feature prominently in the engravings, with human figures and related tools and ornamentation dominating the painted sites.

Dating the art is difficult, though it is likely that the engravings preceded the paintings because of their natural resistance to weathering and flaking. Radiocarbon dating techniques applied to organic matter have been used to date the carbon present in the material utilised in the paints, and place some of the rock art at around 2 700 years old. Paints would have been produced from a variety of resources, including animal blood, ochre, silica, clays and plant extracts.

Assigning meaning to the art has generated, and will continue to provoke, much debate. The San, specifically their spiritual mediums or shamans, are now widely accredited with the bulk of the rock art in southern Africa. Scholars today look to the San spiritual world in an effort to interpret the images and attribute meaning to them. Historically, literal and predominantly Eurocentric interpretations chose to ignore the important spiritual significance of the art to its creators. This has resulted in spectacular misinterpretations, such as the 'White Lady' label attached to the wondrous, penis-adorned image that graces the Brandberg massif. Of all the images, the esoteric geometric patterns and shapes are considered the most difficult to interpret. It is thought they represent visions that shamans encountered whilst in a self-induced state of altered consciousness, or trance. Some of the apparently abstract circular forms are interpreted as games, representations of the sun, or even as maps of natural features, such as waterholes.

Animals represented more than mere sustenance to the San. The giraffe, with its honeycomb-patterned hide, appears to be the most conspicuous engraved image in the North-West, a likely reflection of the importance of this species as a food source for the hunters. Gemsbok, springbok and kudu also feature prominently, with a particularly fine lion, complete with tracks, depicted at Twyfelfontein. Birds are less common, with ostrich and, possibly, flamingos represented. Images of elephant and rhino are particularly prominent in the region, providing a useful historical source of these species' past distribution. Twyfelfontein has some especially fine relief engravings of both these giants.

The future of these precious assets is generally secure, though many sites on private or communal land receive no formal protection other than that offered by landowners or local residents. Looting and vandalism is an unfortunate reality, evidence of the vulnerability of the subject matter. Any protection, however, cannot halt the natural process of erosion and fading that will, inevitably, obliterate all the work.

THE DAMARA PEOPLE

The Damara people have, historically, been cast in the role of the region's pre-historic aboriginal inhabitants. Early European writers invariably identified them as 'Bergdamara', typically characterised as an oppressed people driven to foraging and hunting in the hills. Their Negroid features and Khoe-based language were at odds with colonial racial categorisation, and continue to defy anthropological classification in the post-colonial era. Although they undoubtedly enjoyed close ties with the land, the hunter-gatherer tag is simplistic.

Contemporary rural communities engage in a variety of subsistence activities, with *veldkos,* or bush food, supplementing the produce of their gardens and livestock. Damara women at the small settlement of Khowarib continue to gather grass seeds from the subterranean nests of harvester

Khowarib resident Petrika Ganases excavates the subterranean nest of harvester ants to access the precious grass seeds they store there. She carefully winnows out debris in a purpose-made bowl, before prudently replacing the soil. The seeds are ground into flour and used to make porridge.

ants. Collection of seeds takes place after the rains, by which time the ants have stored a significant cache. A suitable nest is located, and a hole dug to access the seed store. The seeds are then winnowed in a purpose-made wooden bowl, to remove ants and general debris. Great care is taken to minimise disturbance to the nest, with the soil carefully replaced, ensuring the resource is available for future use. The seeds are then taken home for further cleaning before being ground into flour or made into porridge. A beer of seeds, sugar and water is also brewed and honey is still collected from caves, trees and underground sources. However, as with many of the region's cultures and traditions, much of this lore is likely to become distant memory as new generations of sons and daughters are distracted by the variety of commercial foodstuffs available – signalling the inevitable encroachment of the modern world.

A rusty old wreck provides recreation for local children, and, in this case, doubles up as a shop for tourist memorabilia, Damaraland.

DAMARA MIGRATION ROUTES – *Hans Eichab*

From: *The Moon People and other Namibian Stories*

Namibia Oral Tradition Project, New Namibia Books, Windhoek, Namibia, 1996

MANY, MANY YEARS AGO, the forefathers of the people known as the Damaras buried their ancestors in the mountains of West Africa. From three different directions the Damaras moved into Namibia, or South West Africa, as the country was once known.

It is only now that history students attempt to trace the history of the Damara people. Tradition has it that this migration into Namibia had a number of causes. We are told that the first group of Damara trekkers entered the country through Owambo, taking the route between the Kunene and the Okavango. They stayed here for a long time.

Some of the Damara people, we're told, remained in Owambo. They lived between the two rivers, and later spread to the Etosha. In later years, the Ovambos and Hereros found them there. The Damara mingled mostly with the Uukwaludhi and also with the San People.

History teaches that the first group of Damaras entered from eastern Angola. They spread over the places known today as Etosha, Otjitambi, Outjo, Paresis, Okangwe, Twyfelfontein, Fransfontein, Bergsig, Grootberg, Namib, Sesfontein and up to the Kunene River. The tribes were named according to the regions where they lived.

Hereros who settled in Kaokoland, close to the Kunene, came upon the Damaras at Otjitambi. As the Damara people were familiar with the area, they showed the Hereros the places where game and water were plentiful. According to tradition, the first tribes to settle in the area were Muundjuas, Kavaris and Katuoos.

The Damaras at Sesfontein and in the Namib, the Hereros of Kaokoland, and the Ovambo people intermingled easily. Today, these tribes have relatives living across the Kunene River in Angola. The relation between these tribes became clearer during the drought of the 1970s when the cattle of the Uukwaludhi tribe were allowed to graze in Kaoko and the Sesfontein area.

The second group of Damaras crossed five big rivers before they came to a river which is in flood every year – the Okavango. The Damaras stayed there for a short while. However, a conflict, during which the king of the Damaras was killed, developed between them and the neighbouring Ovambos. The Damaras moved further on towards the Omurumba, to Tsumeb, Otavi, Waterberg, Paresis, Erongo and the Khomas region.

The last group of the Damaras (the ¦Gawani¦¦aes) migrated south alongside other Bantu tribes, such as the Shona, Zulu, Xhosa and the Tswanas. It is believed that some of these tribes migrated across the Orange River in the south. The Damaras settled there, and spread as far south as Upington and the Great Karoo, and westwards, to Oranjemund, Warmbad, Hoachanas and Maltahohe. They were among the first people who lived in these places.

They had language of their own in which they sang songs of praise and related stories to their children.

shifting sands

a region in transition

"Change" is scientific, "progress" is ethical; change is indubitable, whereas progress is a matter of controversy.'

Bertrand Russell
Unpopular Essays (1950)
'Philosophy and Politics'

OPPOSITE: Twatuneke Tjingee in thoughtful repose. As matriarch and wife of a headman, she shares some of her husband's responsibilities. Spectacles are an unlikely, but increasingly common, sight amongst the Himba.

LEFT: The colourfully decorated wall of the Herero homestead, Warmquelle.

On the move: a Himba elder complete with head-scratcher, his *ozongwinyu* (wooden pillow) to help maintain his hairstyle, and necklace featuring goats' ears.

TWATUNEKE TJINGEE cuts a striking and gracious figure as wife to the headman of Otjitanda. Body gleaming burnt sienna and dressed in the distinctive Himba attire, it is hard to believe that she is probably well into her seventies. Her only concession to encroaching westernisation is a pair of large, ochre-smudged, horn-rimmed spectacles. These co-ordinate perfectly – intentionally or otherwise – with the rich ochre that symbolises the Himba people and sets them apart from their Herero cousins.

There is something quixotic about the Kunene Region due, in part, to its geographical isolation and the romantic image of its inhabitants. Of all the peoples of Namibia, it is perhaps the Himba who evoke the great-est sense of a bygone era. As traditional cultures fade into print, it is remarkable to find a people who, faced with the Western 'Coca-Cola' juggernaut, have retained many aspects of their rich pastoral culture. Like the robed pastoralists of East Africa, the Himba are often characterised as arrogant and proud. They are, increasingly, the object of intense scrutiny from the outside world, particularly from the burgeoning tourist industry.

The inhabitants of the Kunene have lived, up to the latter part of the 20th century, in what was effectively a national backwater. Now, as the 21st century gathers momentum, they all, and particularly the Himba, face a period of dynamic change, the pace and nature of which will define their place in contemporary Namibia.

THE PAST

It is generally agreed that formal historical documentation of north-west Namibia is limited. Written records of any kind are unavailable prior to the 16th century, and those that exist tend to document events from a Eurocentric and colonial stance. According to historian Michael Bollig, the oral tradition of passing stories from one generation to another has recently experienced a renaissance, gaining recognition as an acceptable and reliable form of recounting historical events in the academic arena. But oral traditions have limited recall and are, by their very nature, open to embellishment and interpretation.

The people of the North-West

Written records indicate that pastoralist Herero people migrated from southern Angola (then Portuguese West Africa) into Kaokoland in the middle of the 16th century, not long after the Ovambo people had settled further to the east. Prevented from moving their cattle into the Etosha area by the powerful Ovambo, the Herero were forced to move westwards to the remote and inhospitable mountainous area of Kaokoland. Widely dispersed springs and waterholes forced these pastoralists of Kaokoland to adopt a semi-nomadic way of life, building scattered and transient settlements. Aridity defined their very existence.

However, after nearly two centuries of trying to eke out a living from the veld, the majority decided to try their luck further south in the more arable area of central Namibia. Those who moved south continued to be known as the Herero, whereas those who remained were later to become known as the Himba.

In the mid-1800s, bands of Swartbooi and Topnaar livestock raiders, a diverse group of Nama and Afrikaans speakers who had fled economic hostility in the Cape colony, began to make incursions into the region. With their superior weaponry and access to horses, this assorted band seized large numbers of livestock throughout Kaokoland and as far afield as southern Angola. By the end of the 19th century, the formerly wealthy cattle herders of the region were reduced to subsisting off the land. These Herero-speaking people became known as the Tjimba, a derogatory term referring to their relatively impoverished state. The word is believed to derive from *ondjimba-ndimba*, meaning aardvark, an animal that is given to digging to procure its food.

A couple of decades later, when the Nama raids were at their worst, many impoverished communities fled into Angola, seeking refuge with the Ngambwe, a related pastoral group. They were not the first to seek protection from the Ngambwe who, with their already over-stretched resources, referred to these refugees as the ovaHimba – those who beg food and shelter. The name stuck.

Vita – a warring hero

It was during this period of instability that the future Herero leader emerged. Vita Tom, known also by the Afrikaans name Oorlog Tom (*vita* meaning 'war' in Herero and *oorlog* meaning 'war' in Afrikaans), was born in Otjimbingwe on

Legendary Herero warrior and leader Vita 'Oorlog' Tom.

Swakop River in 1863. He followed his father, who was in the service of the explorer Frederick Green, to Angola, establishing a reputation as a brave and skilled hunter en route. Under his leadership, the refugees were transformed into a working and fighting force to be reckoned with. They allied themselves to the Portuguese colonialists and the Thirstland Trekkers (groups of Afrikaner farmers, traders and hunters who had settled in southern and central Angola) and started participating in the local economy, exchanging their services – as scouts, labourers, porters and mercenaries – for arms and ammunition. Their forces were further swelled by a group from central Namibia who were fleeing defeat at the hands of Germans during the Herero rebellion.

In 1910 the Portuguese civil administration changed, and the services of the interlopers were no longer needed. Vita Tom and Muhona Katiti, Herero and Himba leaders respectively, were, in effect, leaders of groups of armed mercenaries. With their services surplus to requirement, they channelled their energies instead into conducting raids on neighbouring groups, seizing cattle and accumulating vast herds.

However, a devastating outbreak of the rinderpest (a virulent disease affecting cattle) in the late 1890s wiped out up to 90% of the stolen cattle. On the southern side of the Kunene, Swartbooi and Topnaar raids had finally ceased under a tough German colonial administration, which was endorsing a welcome return to the Kaokoland for the exiles. The rationale of this policy was vague, since German involvement beyond their base at Sesfontein was never very dynamic; apart from exploratory expeditions in search of minerals, the administration had little impact on the people of Kaokoland. Small numbers of Himba started filtering back, building up, finally, to a steady migration. After the German South West African forces surrendered at the end of World War 1, Vita Tom also led his mixed band of followers back to Kaokoland from Angola.

The Dorsland trekkers in the Kunene Region and southern Angola

Meanwhile, another group of people in search of land and autonomy were heading for the Kaokoland – Afrikaner *burghers*, or *trekboers*, from the Transvaal Republic. The hardy Boers who left the Transvaal during the latter part of the 19th century in search of opportunity and a better life led an itinerant existence. The toll exerted on the trekkers was significant, and many succumbed to the rigours of the journey en route as they traversed some of the most inhospitable terrain in the sub-region. They were transients in northwestern Namibia before crossing the Kunene River into Angola (Portuguese West Africa) in 1880. They were to farm and hunt the fertile highlands for nearly sixty years, before returning south after World War 1 to settle finally in what is today known as Namibia (then South West Africa). Their legacy is preserved in graves and monuments that mark their passage, testament to a life defined by profound adversity.

Citing Transvaal President Thomas Burger's lack of religious instruction in schools, and perhaps with an eye on an impending British presence, five groups of dissatisfied boers left the relative safety of the Transvaal Republic between 1874 and 1905. The early trek traversed the Kalahari and skirted the Okavango Delta of present-day Botswana before moving into South West Africa. Crossing the Kalahari, with its long stretches of waterless sandveld, tested both man and beast, and resulted in the Afrikaans epithet 'dorslander', or 'thirstlander', in honour of the hardship encountered. After enduring this, some members chose to settle en route whilst others trekked on, reaching the Etosha Pan in 1878.

From here, a small group of men went ahead on horseback to reconnoitre the land to the west, entering the Kaokoveld for the first

A group of Dorslanders, predominately men and boys, Humpata, Angola, 1898. (National Archives of Namiba)

BELOW: This rather imposing Dorsland monument at Swartbooisdrift, Kunene River, was erected in 1953 to commemorate the return of members of the 1928 trek from Angola. The monument sits on a rise overlooking the humid Kunene River valley.

RIGHT: Like many of her compatriots, sixteen-year-old Danielina Robberts succumbed to the rigours of the journey, and lies on a rise looking over the Kunene River at Swartbooisdrift.

time. Their excursion took them to potential sites of settlement: Sesfontein, Otjitundua and Kaoko Otavi, including a foray down the Skeleton Coast to Rocky Point. They found the relatively favourable conditions at Otjitundua and Kaoko Otavi to their liking and returned to lead the main party there.

To this day, the springs at Kaoko Otavi still provide sustenance to the resident Herero community and their livestock. Leafy sycamore fig trees dwarf the crumbled remains of the church where the settlers once conducted their worship. It is a tranquil location; spring water still ripples down irrigation canals built by the trekkers, channelling the sweet fluid to water crops and livestock. Unmarked graves, not far from the church site, are a reminder of the adversity they endured here.

The trekkers' wanderings in search of a suitable home had taken a considerable toll on their material possessions. The prominent trader and hunter, Axel Eriksson, conceivably prompted by future commercial prospects, wrote to the *Cape Times* in 1879 describing the Boers' now perilous state. In his letter he stated: 'I think it is my duty to inform the public that, on my return journey from Ovampoland (Ovamboland) in May last year, I met at Ocuquca (Okaukuejo) about eighty wagons belonging to these Boers, and saw some six hundred people in a most deplorable state. I might further add, had it not been that these men were good shots, through which means they managed to kill game sufficient to maintain life, they would all have perished long ere this.' The letter raised in excess of £5 000 from concerned burghers at the Cape, and provided the impetus for the move into Angola.

The promise of more arable land to the north meant the Kaokoveld served as only a temporary home for the nearly destitute settlers.

In 1880, the first of these groups crossed the Kunene River into Angola at Tjimuhaka, today's Swartbooisdrift, into Angola. A Baster named William Worthington Jordan, who had previously traded and hunted the area, facilitated their passage north of the Kunene, negotiating with the Portuguese authorities on their behalf. The majority of them settled in Humpata at the foot of the Angolan Highlands. Every family was allocated 200 hectares of land, with an assurance from the Portuguese of religious freedom. Other smaller groups trekked further north to settle. The Earl of Mayo, an English explorer, was an early visitor to Humpata in 1882, and was obviously impressed by what he saw of the community there: 'All the people of the Boer settlement were most kind, obliging and hospitable. A finer set of men I have never seen.'

Beyond a handful of coastal ports, the Portuguese had not developed the interior to any significant degree. The Boers settled a frontier region with the most basic infrastructure. Using their ox-wagons, the settlers soon made an impact on their adopted home, opening a route through the mountains to the port of Mocamedes. This provided a commercially vital link between the coastal anchorages and the fertile interior.

Hunting, particularly for ivory, had become a significant commercial activity in the sub-region because of the scarcity of game further to the south. This had prompted Axel Eriksson's trading company, amongst others, to move their base of operations to the bustling ports of Mocamedes and Porto Alexandre. The Boers had customarily hunted since they were of age, and were soon organised into expeditions that included illegal forays after Kaokoland elephant. Jan Robberts, whose descendants now farm the Outjo District, gained notoriety for leading these intrepid excursions. They undoubtedly contributed to the untimely demise of elephant in much of their northern range.

Elderly Dorsland couple, with bible. (National Archives of Namibia)

With the defeat of Germany in World War 1, South Africa was given a mandate by the League of Nations in 1920 for the control of South West Africa. As part of its policy to effect control on the region, the new South African Administration proceeded, in 1923, to divide Kaokoland into three reserves. These were allocated to Vita Tom (Herero), Muhona Katiti, (Himba), and Kahewa-Nawa, (Tjimba). With around 800 followers, Vita Tom was the most powerful and influential of the leaders.

By 1925 the South African Administration had initiated an exclusionist policy. The border with Angola was controlled, and Portuguese traders were no longer allowed into South West Africa. To the east, trade with the Ovambo was hampered by bureaucracy. Furthermore, large areas between Kaokoland and the farming zone to the south, and Ovamboland to the east, were declared 'neutral' or 'stockfree' with many people forcibly evacuated, including white farmers who had refused the request to move out voluntarily in 1920.

Exodus

Soon the trek wagons were creaking south again on a final journey. Those Boers who had settled in Angola towards the end of the 19th century now started to return, encouraged perhaps by the South African presence in South West Africa, as well as a desire to own the land they tilled. Economic concerns were also central to their decision to leave Angola. The Portuguese currency had crashed in the wake of World War 1, and problems were compounded by the institution of rigorous taxes. Boer children were being forced to attend local schools, where the medium of instruction was Portuguese. The trekkers were perhaps particularly fervent, in exile, on the issue of language, and resolutely opposed this development.

The ODENDAAL COMMISSION

THIS NOTORIOUS BODY WAS APPOINTED in 1962 by the South African Government under the chair of FH Odendaal. Its brief was to look at ways of achieving a policy of separate political development (apartheid) for the various ethnic groups in the then South West Africa. In its report, the Commission proposed a series of homelands, two of which were Damaraland and Kaokoland. Implementation of the Commission's recommendations reduced what was effectively the world's largest game reserve to two much smaller separate entities: the Etosha Game Park and the Skeleton Coast National Park.

The ecological implications of these recommendations were significant, given the reduction of land area holding game conservation status, but, in spite of enormous international criticism, they were implemented in 1970. The area from the Ugab in the south and the Hoanib in the north no longer had any specific legal protection. Furthermore, the Directorate of Nature Conservation had no jurisdiction over the territory. Development of the area was accelerated through the creation of new homeland government infrastructures with inevitable effects on the local economy.

It seemed total folly to designate such marginal habitat as homeland, the greater part of the region having limited agricultural potential. Yet this is what effectively happened and, according to a 1972 survey conducted by the Department of Agriculture, 13 000 cattle-rich pastoralists and an estimated 160 000 cattle, plus small stock, were dependent on the area. A later stock census, conducted by the Directorate of Veterinary Services in 1998, showed that the communal areas of the region north of the veterinary fence were home to more than 170 000 cattle and in excess of 600 000 small stock. Unlike arid-adapted ungulates, which make better use of available resources, thus limiting their impact on their habitat, the introduction of large numbers of domestic livestock has taken its toll. As a result of continuous overgrazing and trampling, especially around watering points, whole areas have degenerated into virtual dustbowls, Sesfontein being a perfect example.

A delegation found a sympathetic hearing from the Union government in Cape Town, which agreed to fund the repatriation. Land was allocated and financial aid was given to settle the nearly 2 000 trekkers in South West Africa. They crossed the Kunene River in 1928, exchanging their wagons for motorised transport provided by the government. After a brief spell in transit camps, they left for farms in the Gobabis, Outjo and Kamanjab districts, many of which proved to be sited on marginal agricultural land. In spite of this, the trekkers had finally found a home amongst fellow Afrikaners. The wagons would roll no more.

Tightening the screws

Under South African control, the Kaokoland had become a district in its own right. However, in an effort apparently aimed at controlling the Namibian meat market in favour of white farmers, the authorities went to great lengths to monitor stock movement in the region, forbidding the movement of cattle, particularly from Angola. In 1948, with an outbreak of foot-and-mouth disease, Kaokoland was declared a quarantine zone and all livestock trade was prohibited, further isolating the territory from the central market. Lifted partially in 1948, the ban still prohibited livestock marketing outside the region and continues today: all livestock must be quarantined for 21 days prior to export south of the fence.

Bollig argues that, with no opportunity to operate beyond the borders of their region on account of these imposed restrictions, the people of Kaokoland had little choice but to resort, once more, to a subsistence economy. Their interlude as participants in an evolving local economy (as hunters, traders, labourers, trackers, mercenaries, etc.) was short-lived and the pastoralists of Kaokoland were once again compelled to rely on 'traditional' livestock skills as their sole means of survival. Without the means to generate a cash income, Kaokolanders were excluded from participation in the formal economy, effectively removing all 'development' opportunities and preventing them from integrating into the national market.

Divide and rule

Further change came in the early sixties with the creation of the Odendaal Commission and a proposed series of 'homelands' where each ethnic group could progress towards so-called autonomous administration. These proposals were accepted and resulted in the setting up of two national homelands – Kaokoland and Damaraland – in 1970. Development of the area accelerated with the creation of the new homeland government infrastructures and social services, all of which had an unavoidable effect on the economy of the region. 'Westernisation' had finally arrived. However, although access to education and medical facilities became available, few people, and the Himba especially, attended school until the 1980s.

This imposing Dorsland monument at Swartbooisdrift, on a rise overlooking the humid Kunene River valley, was erected in 1953 to commemorate the return of members of the 1928 trek from Angola.

Survival

The verdant, palm-lined banks of the Kunene River are home to four generations of Afrikaners. The Grobbelar family operates a tourist lodge at Swaartbooisdrift, a remote, yet historically significant outpost. 'Oom Grobbie' is the family patriarch, born at Mombolo in what was Portuguese West Africa (Angola) in 1926. He was two years old when his family joined the exodus back to the then South West Africa, assembling at Swaartbooisdrift in 1928. His abiding memory of the return trip was a failed attempt by his father to shoot an elephant that had crossed the track, out of rifle range. His mother did not return from Angola, having succumbed to fever after falling into a river fully clothed.

His father was one of thousands of Afrikaners who farmed, traded and hunted the southern Angolan bounty. A handful of other 'Angola Boere' have survived in the region, and have a wealth of tales to tell of their time in the verdant territory to the north.

'Without doubt, during that terrible journey, it was a case of the survival of the fittest.'

English explorer, The Earl of Mayo, 1882

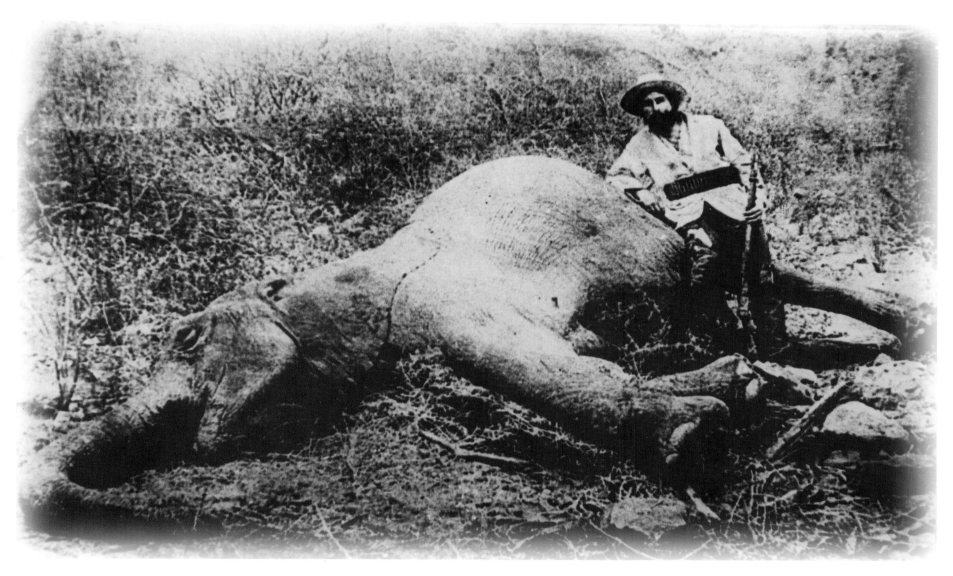

William James Bushnell Chapman, son of the famous explorer and pioneer photographer James Chapman, was a trader and hunter who accompanied the Dorsland trek to Angola; here he is photographed with an elephant he shot in southern Angola, circa 1895. (National Archives of Namibia)

WILLEM JACOBUS PRINSLOO ALBERTS
Dorslandtrekker, Outjo

'Oom Willie', as he is known, still dons a hat when visitors drop in to Bougainvillaea, his well-tended home in sleepy Outjo. Alberts is a name synonymous with the exploits of the various treks that left South Africa on their often arduous journeys north. His grandfather, Gert, is credited with leading two parties of trekkers, including a reconnaissance party on horseback, which surveyed much of present-day Kaokoland. Oom Willie's brother Andries, a writer, has documented much of the 'Angola-Boere' tales in his *'In Vreemdelingskap'*.

'Change seems to come quickly now.

Everything I've seen in my life has been eclipsed

by developments of the last 10 years.'

ON LIFE IN ANGOLA . . .

I was born in Mombolo, Portuguese West Africa on the 29th August 1919. I'm one of four children. My grandparents trekked to Angola from South Africa to find a better life. My grandfather, Gert Alberts, was one of the original trek leaders. They settled for a brief time in the Etosha area, where my grandmother died. Her grave still stands near the Rietfontein waterhole in the park. They then moved north looking for better country to settle. Angola was a green land with water everywhere. You could grow anything. My grandfather was one of the first teachers, although he'd had no training. His first month's salary came in the form of a hat! Later, teachers were sent from churches in South Africa. A young teacher by the name of Hennie Venter stands out in my mind. He was handicapped, with a clubfoot, I think, and travelled on a donkey, visiting families in the district. My father farmed corn and vegetables, and hunted game to sell the hides. He had two wagons, one for transport and another, which the family used to sleep in when we were on the move.

ON TREKKING BACK . . .

My mother didn't want to leave Angola. She was quite content there. We had a nice house and had acquired beautiful furniture from Portugal. However, the land was never ours – the work was yours but the property wasn't. The Portuguese also taxed us heavily and wanted us to integrate into their schools. My older brother learnt Portuguese, but the schools were closed before I had the opportunity. Over 300 families decided to return. The ox wagons were heavily laden for the journey. Ours included my mother's organ, which she refused to leave behind. She'd never had lessons but played beautifully in spite of that. The going was slow, there were no roads, and we often got stuck in the sand. My mother saw this as a sign that we weren't supposed to leave. I remember the clear water and the stones on the river bottom when we crossed. The Kunene was very low. Because of veterinary restrictions we had to sell all our livestock before crossing over. We then travelled in trucks provided by the state.

ON LIFE IN SOUTH WEST AFRICA . . .

After we arrived from Angola, we stayed for a few weeks at a transit camp near Outjo called Gamgarab. We lived in tents. I was ten years old when I went to school for the first time. Families were then allocated farms around the country. Some went to Grootfontein, others to the Gobabis area. My father yearned to be closer to Angola, so settled on a farm near Kamanjab, called Kamanjab 'C'. My parents and grandmother on my mother's side (Prinsloo) are all buried on the farm. My granddaughter and her husband still live there, and continue to farm.

ON HIS LIFE . . .

Change seems to come quickly now. Everything I've seen in my life has been eclipsed by developments of the last 10 years. Morals have slipped; television is full of adultery and violence. I fear for the future. I was a farmer all my life: cattle and karakul sheep too. The prices used to be good for their pelts. I've never been one to move around a lot. My brother became a writer and moved away from farming. I've lived here all my life and will die here. If I had to do it all over again I would farm karakul again – I wouldn't change a thing.

Transition: an intriguing fusion of Himba refinement and European football culture, Enyandi, 2000.

'Today the Himba people do not need to be encouraged to stay "traditional", however quaint, simple and attractive such a lifestyle appears to jaded city dwellers. What the Himba do need is continued rights to their own land and water, the right to control their resources and most of all, the freedom to choose their own destiny as citizens of Namibia.'

Dr Margaret Jacobsohn: *Himba – Nomads of Namibia*, 1990

THE PRESENT

Thousands of tourists visit the Kunene region every year, looking to make contact with the local people. The Himba have become one of the main attractions for these visitors who come brandishing sophisticated cameras in their quest for images depicting a 'lost' and more 'traditional' way of life.

Young boys have their hair fashioned into *ondatu* (single plaits) down the back of the head with the rest of their hair shaved off. Young men increasingly use modern fabrics to decorate the *ondatu* and create an individual style. In early adulthood, the *ondatu* is split in two, signalling that a young man is ready to marry.

KOZONGOMBE TJINGEE
Headman, Otjitanda

Tjingee is a senior headman, presiding over a significant portion of north-west Kaokoland. His homestead at Otjitanda, set amongst attractive wooded highlands, is too remote to warrant a store. From here, he presides over a substantial accumulation of cattle, goats and sheep. Tjingee is in his early eighties. Age has rendered him a wizened, elfin figure with a myriad of aches. As an elder, he is entitled to relate the oral traditions of his group, which he does with eloquent authority.

ON HISTORY AND FAMILY . . .

I was born at Otjizu not far from here. I got my title from my father, Kakuruouye, who was a great warrior in the time of the Germans and Namas. He had a big gun, ombandururwa, given to him by the Germans. He fought and raided cattle all over this land and into Angola. When the English came he brought his people from Angola and settled here. Our people are all buried (in a place) not far from here. Only the men are buried together. The women must be buried in another place. This is our tradition. The war here (liberation war) was bad for our people as many were killed and lost their cattle. People fled to the towns for protection from the army. Some of our people fled to Angola and are still there today. The war was bad as it divided our people.

ON CATTLE . . .

In the dry time, when our cattle died, we had to travel far – to Okarara (near Otjiwarongo) – to replenish our herds. The war was also bad for our cattle as people fled to the towns for security, leaving their cattle behind. There was no one to look after them and many were killed. If all our cattle die then we die. Without cattle we have no future. We have certain sacred cattle that we cannot eat. If we use them we will all die. Ours are a golden brown colour. I might give these away or exchange them because we can't use them.

Kozongombe Tjingee at the Holy Fire. The milk collected at the daily milking ceremony cannot be consumed by anyone until the headman has completed the *makera* ritual at the Holy Fire.

ON THE HOLY FIRE (*OKURUWO*) . . .

We will keep the Holy Fire here at Otjitanda, it's important for us. Without it we're lost and will die. Others may choose to leave the Holy Fire, this depends on the individual. Some are proud of their culture and others not. I believe we'll continue to use it here at Otjitanda.

ON WILDLIFE . . .

In the past, we had many animals until the white men came and took them away to their parks. You could see everything in this area: lion, elephant, rhino, and antelope. In the past our ancestors took (hunted) as they needed, as we did. Now we can be caught and go to jail even if we take one kudu. We only see them (conservation officials) when they want to arrest us. The conservancy is a good thing if we're not arrested and can hunt some animals.

ON SCHOOL . . .

I was responsible for the school here. My cattle paid for its construction. I'm happy to have a school in the area. Education is important for the future. We also need a store here; it's a long way for us to get to a store. We hope someone will build one soon.

ON TOURISTS . . .

People often drive past without greeting us. This isn't good. They should at least greet us and acknowledge us. This is our home.

ON THE FUTURE . . .

I have seven children. Unfortunately I have only one son amongst them, so I really have only one child. He'll succeed me as headman and my brother, Ruhara Muhenje, will continue to serve as a councillor. The future depends on the rains, if they come.

LEFT: As a boy approaches puberty, and after circumcision, he will begin to wear the *ombware* – a white bead necklace made by his mother. As he matures, further layers of beads will be added to thicken the *ombware*. This is likely to be one of the first traditions to die amongst young Himba men.

BELOW: The encroachment of western commodities is evident in this temporary shelter. Alcohol abuse is a growing problem amongst the Himba of north-west Namibia.

OPPOSITE: The mural on this house highlights the fact that elephant are never far from the community (Khowarib).

Agents of change

Juxtaposed with this adherence to a traditional lifestyle, however, is the current reality of the 21st century with its mood of technology-fuelled advancement. By the end of the 20th century, ten years of independence and an assertive development policy to bring the Kunene Region into line with the 'modern' world have resulted in a dynamic mood of change for its inhabitants.

Central government seeks to integrate all ethnic groups into a common society and economy, with boundaries that were construed as 'ethnic' being redrawn. Kaokoland and Damaraland have been subsumed to form the political district of Kunene, and although Opuwo has been designated the new capital of the

region, it remains something of a backwater, still without a bank.

The Himba people find themselves at odds with the modern political state. Their loyalty to their own socio-economic system still ranks them among the most economically independent, albeit 'traditional', of Namibia's people. This 'traditionalism', however, is seen by many to obstruct development and progress. As the cash economy permeates further into the pastoral realm, mass-produced goods have become more readily available. By the end of the 20th century, even the most remote settlements had blankets, cooking pots and other utensils. Most Himba men today own one or more items of western clothing – a shirt or jacket of some kind – and T-shirts have been *de rigeur* in some areas since the mid-1980s.

The agents of change that have had the greatest impact on the Himba in the modern age are education, wage labour and tourism. Subsequently, many young people now have a vision of their future beyond the perimeter of the *onganda* (homestead). Increasingly, their experiences outside the confines of this world are producing new aspirations, causing them to question their traditions and social structures. As with any culture however, tradition is not, and never has been, static.

The *onganda* (homestead)

Visitors are often perplexed by the fact that, in a climate where temperatures regularly exceed 40°C, local people should choose to build their *ongandas* in the open, with no shade. For the seasoned inhabitants of the North-West, it is simple logic that dictates the location of a settlement or transitory camp. Heavily wooded sites are avoided as they make ideal sanctuaries for dangerous wildlife, particularly those with a predilection for livestock. Trees and shrubs are also home to a greater number of potentially harmful snakes, scorpions and ticks.

Opposite: Herero houses differ from Himba houses in that they are rectangular, and generally more substantial.

frames, consequently having more of an impact on natural resources and generally being more permanent. Herero women have largely lost their role as house builders and depend mainly on their men for construction.

Unlike the contemporary Herero man who plays an integral role in the building of his home, a Himba man is forbidden from participating in this task. Traditionally, he cannot even attain full adult status without a wife. He cannot officiate at a sacred fire unless he is married, nor will his matrilineage hand over stock until he has a wife. Without the essential support of a wife, he cannot become a successful herder and his wealth has little meaning without heirs. Finally, and perhaps most crucially, a Himba man cannot acquire a 'proper' house without a wife to handle the cattle dung-and-earth plaster necessary to cement a home.

The layout of both Himba and Herero homesteads comes from the same blueprint. The cattle *kraal* and the Holy Fire are the hub of any homestead, but the dwellings are different. The main houses and all other dwellings in a Himba homestead are built by the women. The houses are invariably round with a central pole, utilising minimal resources. Herero houses, on the other hand, are more substantial structures. They are rectangular, with no central pole, and require more wood and sturdier

ABOVE: To the semi-nomadic Himba, an empty
house or homestead is not abandoned.

LEFT: Wet-season home.

RIGHT: People and cattle
live in quiet harmony.

The significance of the *onganda*, like many other aspects of daily life, is undergoing change. Before the drought and the bush war, an independent prestige system for both men and women existed. As the process of modern rule in the North-West progressed, a council of headmen was established, which met in Opuwo – thereby effectively excluding the majority of women from attending. In spite of this, the *onganda* continued to remain the economic centre for most communities until the 1980s. But established roles were being eroded. By participating in council meetings, the headman's status and influence in the community greatly exceeded his earlier socio-judicial role. As a member of the council, he was effectively representing his people at State level.

Dual descent

Himba and Herero communities both organise their social structures according to the principle of dual descent. Practised in only a handful of other cultures worldwide, every individual in the community is linked to two completely distinct groups of relatives. One line of descent is traced through the female descendants of the mother – the matriclan or *eanda* – and the other through the male descendants of the father – the patriclan or *oruzo*. Each clan fulfils separate roles, and within both matriclans and patriclans there are distinct lineages of people who are directly related.

The main authority within a family group is organised according to patriclan principles and has jurisdiction over, amongst other things, religious activities and location of residence. Whereas the patriclan has much

The MATRICLAN

'Significant' relatives are those from the same matriclan. Individuals who share the same matriclan will have very close ties with their maternal relatives – their mother's brothers and sisters.

A woman will formally adopt the patriclan of her husband in a special ceremony after they are married, but she will retain, as will her husband, her matriclan for life.

An intricate calf-skin head-dress, the erembe, *denotes Twatuneke Tjingee's status as a married woman. It is removed only during periods of mourning.*

If a woman is widowed, she will invert the erembe *to indicate her new status.*

greater daily influence on an individual, it is the matriclan that carries the greater social weight. Major economic control and the inheritance of moveable assets and wealth are organised according to matriclan principles. A son, therefore, does not inherit material wealth or property from his father, but from his uncle (his mother's brother). He does, however, inherit his father's position as lineage head.

Based on the belief that all Himba and Herero are born into one of seven matriclans (originating through a single female ancestor whose daughters and granddaughters founded the different matriclans), membership of the matriclan is considered of supreme importance. It takes precedence over, but does not negate the importance of, the patriclan, which has no tradition of a common origin for all. As with the matriclans, no one patriclan is considered of higher rank or importance than another. The only exception to this rule is the hereditary leadership position which is passed down through either of the two clans.

More recently, however, new economic and social realities have become evident. In a few areas, matrilineal inheritance has been superseded by patrilineal inheritance, with

Himba men expose their hair only during periods of mourning. This sometime resident of Orupembe has acquired a woollen sweater to keep out the cold mornings.

The PATRICLAN

The patriarch, or lineage head, of a family is responsible for the day-to-day running of a homestead. Sole authority rests with him and is hereditary.

Each patriclan has unique and idiosyncratic rules, which were imposed by a founding ancestor. These often involve prohibitions on the ownership or consumption of certain cattle or small livestock, usually based on colour. Different clans will exchange beasts that do not conform to their rules.

Some clans have rules determining which direction the *kraal* (fenced enclosure) faces; others consider certain animal parts, meat or other foods, taboo.

cattle being raised for market or as commodities for exchange. Since economic method is influenced by external forces, it makes more sense for wealth to be passed directly from father to son rather than through an uncle who may live hundreds, if not thousands, of kilometres away, with completely different economic and social pressures. As a cash economy becomes increasingly the norm, this trend is likely to continue.

Cattle country

There are those who believe that the semi-nomadic Himba represent a way of life that no longer has any place in modern Namibia. The perception of the 'traditional' Himba, whose observance of customary markers such as dress and ornamentation place them in another era, is often contrasted with that of the Herero people, who are perceived as being more 'modern', 'progressive' and 'integrated' than their Himba cousins. However, whilst one group may appear more in kilter with the modern age, the two are part of a common culture from shared roots, as evidenced by their shared language and customs.

One of the most significant tenets of this is the common adherence to the 'cattle culture', a pastoralist ethic that is central to their identity as a people. Cattle, goats and sheep are the currency of the Himba and Herero residents of the Kunene region, regardless of their degree of westernisation. This economic specialisation is refined by semi-nomadic habits that optimise resource utilisation in an often harsh and unpredictable environment. It determines when and where they move their stock, and for how long they reside in an area.

Namibia is home to a number of imported cattle breeds, but the indigenous Sanga cattle, representing roughly one fifth of the country's population, are found predominantly north of the veterinary cordon fence that divides Kaokoland from the southern extremity of the Kunene Region. This excludes communal residents and farmers north of the fence from the main commercial livestock markets to the south and forms a boundary between primarily subsistence-based pastoralism and commercial farming.

'If all our cattle die then we die.'

Kozongombe Tjingee,
Headman, Otjitanda

There are thought to be 36 categories of sacred cattle, each one named and identified by its coloration – in this case, *ondorokondo*, which is a term referring to any animal with patchy markings. Whilst the sacred cattle belong to the patriline, the rest of the herd belong to the matriline of the head of the household.

The communal farmers of the North-West require animals that can survive in harsh conditions and *Sanga*, the collective name for the various indigenous breeds of southern African cattle, are ideally suited to the rigours of life in the arid environment. Commercial farmers recognise their value for crossbreeding purposes because their inherent resistance to parasites and drought makes them robust and highly successful breeders.

Although the Himba and Herero have been ranked amongst some of the wealthiest stockowners in Namibia, and indeed Africa, their economy is not based purely on the produce of their herds and flocks. Whilst cattle and smallstock provide the food staples of milk, meat and raw materials for daily necessities (clothing, bedding, shelter, ornaments, utensils etc.), supply varies seasonally. Milk, a staple, is available in sufficient quantities throughout the year for only the wealthiest stockowners, and dry-season supplements are necessary in the form of vegetable crops, wild plants and game meat. Some communities engage in a limited form of furrow-irrigated horticulture as a dietary supplement

These pastoral nomads have survived into modern times because they have evolved lifestyles and practices that are responsive to the arid terrains they inhabit. However, even the most traditional communities are selectively adopting and adapting to certain aspects of modern western culture. Innovations such as boreholes have altered the natural order both socially and environmentally, impacting far beyond the reduction in stock movements that was previously necessary. The seasonal search for pasture has gradually evolved into a more sedentary system.

ABOVE: *Ehoro*, the traditional wooden milk pail, is often nowadays replaced with tin and plastic containers.

RIGHT: Babies are carried around in an *ondikwa* made from calf's leather.

With the demise of most of the region's predators in the 1960s and 1970s, one of the main roles of young men has become redundant, since continuous daily herding is no longer necessary. There is also the increasing lure of wage labour. Young men are likely to spend more time away, engaged in or seeking work. They are not available to move stock when necessary and children, who traditionally work as goatherds till puberty,

The MILKING RITUAL

It is early morning and the women of Kozongombe Tjingee's homestead allow the cows back into the central *kraal*. They have been banished outside the main enclosure overnight, their calves kept in a small internal *kraal* within the main *kraal*, which surrounds the beehive-shaped huts of the family. The calves call plaintively to their mothers, for they are hungry. The children of the *kraal* are also in attendance as able assistants and apprentices in this daily ritual. One by one, the calves are allowed out, rushing immediately to the source of their sustenance. A small brown-and-white calf with a headstrong demeanour is followed languidly by one of the women carrying a thong, a stick and a fashioned wooden milk pail. After being allowed a brief suckle, the calf is brushed aside. The thong is fastened around the back legs of the cow, temporarily immobilising it. The stick is used to keep the hungry and frus-

trated calf at bay. All this is achieved without spilling a precious drop of milk. When the pail has been filled and the milk is taken away, ready for the next stage of the ritual, the calf is allowed to quench its thirst. This process is repeated, until all the cows have been milked and all the calves have been fed. The calves are then herded back into the central *kraal*, while the cows file away to graze and water for the day.

This scene is enacted every morning in Otjitanda and is a reminder of the fact that strict homage is still paid to the daily milking rites in many of the homesteads throughout the region. The milk-tasting ritual takes place at the Holy Fire, where the patriarch asks his ancestors to free the milk from any taboos, making it available for general consumption.

The Himba dig holes in the sandy river beds to access subterranean water for themselves and for their livestock.

been performed. The meat is only eaten during traditional ceremonies, of which funerals and commemoration rituals are the most important occasions in the Himba tradition.

As village head and the oldest member of his own patrilineal group, Kozongombe Tjingee has a myriad of responsibilities within his homestead. It is one of his duties to ensure that the Holy Fire – or *Okuruwo* – is maintained. Every morning, and at dusk each evening, the Holy Fire is tended to ensure that the embers constantly smoulder, ready to be encouraged into flame for important ceremonies or rituals. The chore of keeping the embers alive usually falls to the women of the homestead, often the wife of the headman.

The Holy Fire is seen as the only tangible link between the living and the dead. Himba and Herero cultures both remain faithful to the idea that through the ritual fire they can communicate with the ancestors of their patrilineal kin group. Each homestead has its own ritual fire, always positioned between the door of the main dwelling and the entrance to the central kraal. Traditionally, no social, cultural or economic activity can take place without the ancestors being called to bear witness at the Holy Fire. However, whilst still an important part of the Himba/Herero heritage, it is no longer being observed as widely as before.

may be at school. A direct result of these labour shortages is reduced herding skills, reduced mobility of stock and less effective herd management with the consequent negative impact on the environment.

Sacred cattle

For both Himba and Herero, the most important possessions of any patriline are their sacred cattle – *ozongombe zoviruru*. Whilst the sacred cattle belong to the patriline, the rest of the herd belongs to the matriline of the head of the household. The cattle are identified according to their coloration and marking and the milk of these cows cannot be consumed by anyone until the ritual at the Holy Fire, the *makera*, has

Making sure that the cattle

are heading for home.

CATTLE COLOURS

Some of the more common colorations

Courtesy of Kuva Rutari

ONDOOZU (Bull) OSAONA (Cow)	All Black
OSAAZU (Bull)	All Red
ONDUMBU	All Butter
OMBAPA	All White
OMBONGORA	Black with white collar
EKONDO	Red with white belly
ONDANGA	Red with white blaze
OMBAWE	Red with white patches
EKUNDE	Red brindle
ONDOROKONDO	Any patchy cattle
OHAKA	Red with white belly
OMBAMBI	Black-brown
ONDJANDJA	Brindle

Burial

As with all notable ceremonies, the Holy Fire plays an integral role in the death and burial of a village head. With his death, the effective link between living and dead members of the patriclan is severed and the organisation of the Holy Fire is affected. According to custom, the death of the village or *kraal* head causes the Holy Fire to lose its sacred properties and a complicated series of rituals must then be followed as the old village head is buried and the new head takes his place. With the succession of a new patriarch, the Holy Fire is restored along with its link to the ancestral spirits.

The funeral, in addition to being an important ceremony to celebrate and honour the deceased, is the focal point for a gathering of the clans. Often, people have to travel great distances – no small feat in a region characterised by poor roads and limited access to transport. The lengthy ritual of burial affords an opportunity for far-flung relatives and communities to interact. Many issues are inevitably discussed at such momentous gatherings. Outstanding problems are resolved,

decisions concerning migration routes are made and marriages are arranged. All of this intense social activity is intrinsic to the ceremony and ritual, celebrating death and the ancestors. It is a tangible display of respect, not only for the deceased but also for the heirs and descendants of the patriline. After the deceased has been buried, relatives and guests gather for the extended celebration lasting as long as two months. A number of prize cattle are slaughtered to provide meat and copious amounts of maize and alcohol will be provided for the gathering, often attended by hundreds of people.

When a young man marries, his hair is fashioned into a thick roll on top of his head and worn in an *ondumba*, a soft piece of leather or black cloth covering his hair.

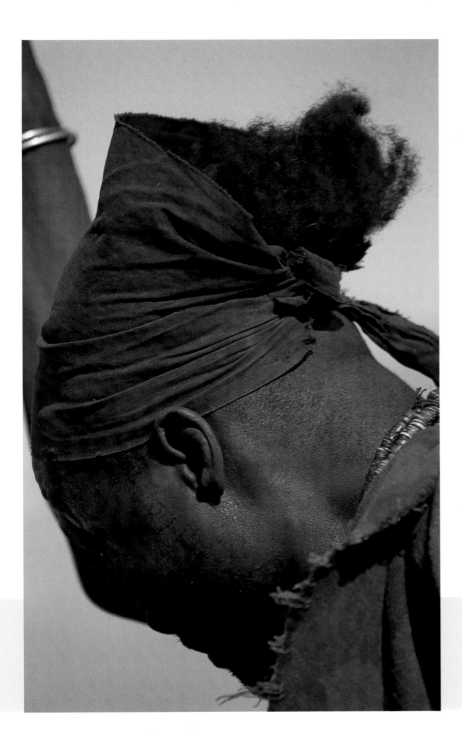

Relatives adopt special hairstyles, wearing certain clothing and ornaments to show that they are in mourning. Women remove their elaborate head ornaments, the *erembe*, traditionally made from calves' leather. A widow will replace her headwear only after the appropriate period of mourning, and then wear it inside out to signify her loss. She will also wear a necklace of beads made of ostrich shell to signify her status as a widow. Men who are directly related to the deceased also bare their heads – protocol dictating that they never appear in public without the traditional *ondumbu* (headwear) at any other time – exposing a shock of hair. They cover their heads again a year later, once they have revisited the grave.

After the year has passed, relatives and guests return to the grave for the first commemoration ceremony. The entire herd of the deceased is brought from even the most distant cattle post. Principal members of the gathering are then presented at the Holy Fire, after which the entire party visits the grave, together with a large portion of the herd. At the end of the ceremony a fire is lit at the foot of the grave and ashes from the fire are taken back to the homestead to the Holy Fire. This is when inheritance matters are settled. Wives, children and herds are formally given into the care of the heir who is introduced at the Holy Fire as successor to the deceased.

If a man appears bareheaded in public, it is a sign of disrespect to the ancestors, but if a relative dies the *ondumba* must be removed for several months to signify the state of mourning. Until recently, all married men kept their heads covered except during this period.

OKURUWO – *the Holy Fire of the Hereros*

McMarvin Katunghange

Abridged from *'The Moon People and other Namibian Stories'*

Namibia Oral Tradition Project, New Namibia Books, Windhoek, Namibia, 1996

HEREROS STRONGLY BELIEVE that the Holy Fire can solve their problems because, through it, they communicate with their ancestors. The Holy Fire has been with the Herero people since time immemorial. Herero chiefs like Hosea Kutako, Tjamahua and many others used it when they fought against the Germans and the Namas.

The use of the Holy Fire differs from Herero to Herero. Just as some Hereros dislike bareheaded cattle, others dislike cattle with horns. Some Hereros turn to the Fire frequently, others consult it only in times of great need. But all Hereros believe that the Holy Fire is the only powerful element through which their problems can be solved – in the same way that Christians believe that Christ can solve their problems.

The Holy Fire is the Foundation, Assembly and Union of the Hereros. The Holy Fire has certain rules, for example that the man is the head of the house, and that as the head he is the one who communicates with the ancestors. When he dies, his older or younger brother takes over the running of the Holy Fire. Also, the Holy Fire must be attended early in the morning and at dusk. It is kept alive through a small piece of burning wood taken to it every day before sunrise and again just before sunset. When there are women about, it is the women who tend to the fire; boys and girls are not allowed to take the burning wood to the Holy Fire. The Holy Fire is permanently situated between the house and the *kraal*. The Hereros believe it is very important to keep in close contact with their ancestors and to pass the tradition on to the younger generation.

And so the Holy Fire keeps the Herero people in close touch with what is happening around them, and what direction their lives must take. It is important to keep the Holy Fire alive among us.

The connection between the Holy Fire and graves signifies the harmonious relationship between the ancestors and their living descendants and is considered crucial to the well-being of the remaining members of the household. The grave will be visited again at subsequent remembrance ceremonies, although the frequency of visits will decline with time. All permanent settlements have at least one graveyard. People are generally buried near where they settled during their latter years, but are sometimes buried in their birthplace or at a site they considered special. Traditionally, chiefs were buried in the community graveyard, but recently the trend has been to bury them apart. Men are buried separately from women; a son will generally be buried alongside his father and at a distance from his mother and siblings.

LEFT: This display of oxen skulls mounted at the grave is an indication of the deceased's wealth and standing in the community. In the middle of the 20th century other signs of wealth and status started to emerge in the form of western-style gravestones, with carvings symbolising the character and standing of the deceased.

BELOW: The engravings on this 'modern' headstone indicate the hunting skills of the deceased – having killed an elephant and a lion – and highlight the fact that he was a soldier.

Whilst religious beliefs and rituals attached to death and burial have remained fairly intact, the decoration of graves has, inevitably, changed over time. Graves were traditionally decorated with stones – *ozondongo* – the affluence of the deceased being denoted by their number and quality. A display of oxen skulls mounted at the grave also displayed wealth and standing in the community. During the 1940s and 1950s the style of decoration changed. Skulls continue to feature prominently, but other signs of wealth and status have been incorporated in the form of expensive, western-style gravestones with carvings symbolising the character and standing of the deceased.

According to Himba belief, a grave symbolises something more than the place where a person's remains are buried. Graves are important for determining social relationships and relationships with the land. They are also the focal point for important religious rituals. As settlement patterns change, so too does the selection of a graveyard's location. They are usually located near a watercourse, often under large trees. Riparian locations are preferable for both practical and symbolic reasons: they are the places where communities traditionally congregate and where key events and discussions take place. The physical existence of a grave is not in itself important, but the connection between the grave and a family's history, the community's system of land-tenure and their decision-making is what is significant.

A graveyard documents the history of a community; more importantly, graves also determine 'ownership' of land and resources. The 'owner' of the land is, in most cases, the oldest male member of a family that has lived in the area for generations. Such claims are founded on the number of graves and generations of ancestors in the area. By demonstrating a long connection with the land, an individual will be afforded respect and authority which is key in land-related issues.

Less remote communities have seen the demise of some of the old ways, although the relative isolation of some settlements has acted as a deterrent to many of the extrinsic influences that have brought these changes. However, planned infrastructural developments for the area may soon change the daily routine in even the most far-flung homestead.

THE FUTURE
The development dilemma

The construction of dams has become a controversial exercise in an environmentally sensitised era, with social and environmental impacts increasingly an integral component of the pre-construction feasibility process. The Lower Kunene Hydropower Scheme is a case in point. It has thus far proved true to script, pitting resident Himba communities and environmentalists against the State in an increasingly acrimonious encounter. Although the scheme was first proposed by German colonists in the 1890s, the current proposal is based on a South African and Portuguese blueprint from 1969, and reflects the dilemma presented by projects of similar scope elsewhere in the world. Zimbabwe's Tonga people, for example, suffered considerable social trauma after they were relocated from the Zambezi Valley to make way for the Kariba dam. With this scenario in mind, opponents of the Kunene dam cite social, cultural and environmental considerations that counter the ostensible economic necessity of the project.

The Namibian government is keen to promote energy self-sufficiency, maintaining that surplus power could be sold to countries in the sub-region. Moreover, the project is seen as a prestigious undertaking that will provide much-needed, albeit temporary, employment during the construction phase.

The picturesque Epupa Falls on the Kunene River, one of two proposed sites for a controversial hydropower scheme.

Critics of the dam dispute its viability, given the projected financial costs. Cost and time overruns, as well as inflated estimates of future national demand for electricity, are primary deficiencies highlighted in the project's feasibility study. The social impact on the Himba culture is cited, too, as a largely neglected human aspect of the study. The dam will displace over 100 Himba dwellings, and inundate nearly 200 ancestral graves – central to a number of Himba traditions, as already discussed. Vocal critic of the scheme, Himba headman Hikuminue Kapika, has a grandfather buried on the bank of the river and does not want to lose this aspect of his heritage.

The waterfalls at Epupa – a popular tourist attraction – would disappear under the dam waters, impacting on a valued source of revenue for local residents. The loss of riverine habitat, which the Himba rely on for dry-season pasture, and the impact of the dam on downstream river ecology complete a rather bleak scenario.

Alternative energy sources to meet Namibia's future needs have been suggested, including power from South Africa (currently utilised), gas-produced power and relatively expensive wind and solar options. The motive, however, for the government's apparent resolve to see Epupa built lies partly in the politicization of the project. Some see it as a gesture of authority over this traditional opposition-party stronghold. The Windhoek regime has also variously described the Himba as 'primitive' and 'backward'. They are, at best, viewed as an embarrassment to a 'vision' of a modern, urban Africa.

One cannot deny that the region has received few benefits from post-independence economic development. Business interests in the regional capital Opuwo are, therefore, understandably enthusiastic supporters of the project. They argue that the scheme will inject much-needed capital into the stagnant regional economy. However, with no foreign financial aid forthcoming, and wavering Angolan commitment to the Epupa site, the dam remains a controversial and uncertain venture.

The challenge ahead

The dam epitomises the dilemma faced by the Himba – the challenge of retaining essential elements of their culture, whilst adapting to, and participating in, the dynamic 'new world' that confronts their sons and daughters. The disappearance of obvious markers such as traditional attire must not be interpreted as signalling the impending demise of the culture. Rather, the disruption of their enduring pastoral tradition is a genuine threat to these people: wither the herds, then wither the Himba.

Contemporary Himba men are increasingly discarding their 'traditional' attire for 'western' fashion. As participants in the formal economy, they have an opportunity to reinvent their image. Illustrating this dichotomy, community game guard Kuva Rutari shares a joke with a friend.

behemoths

large mammals in an unlikely setting

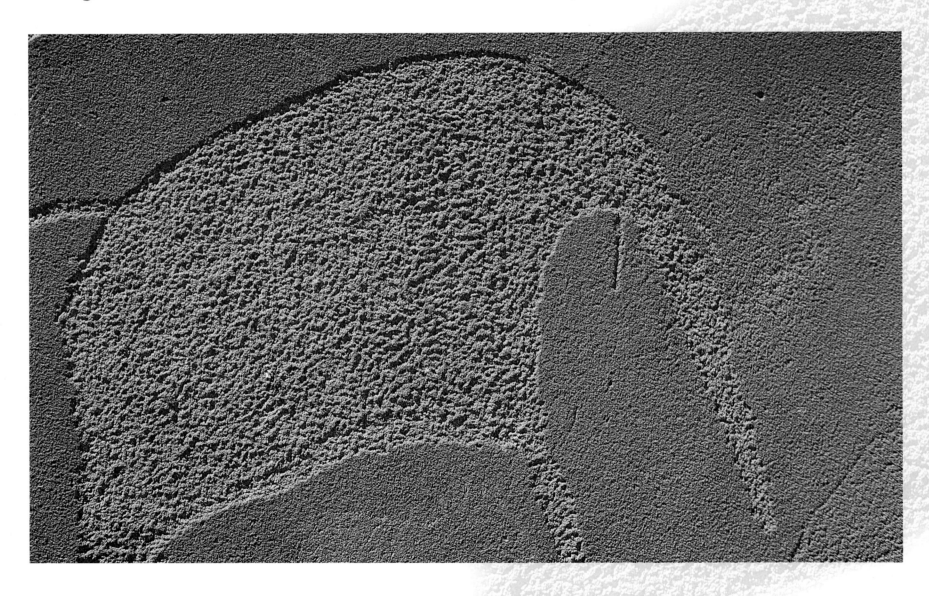

'. . . the prosperity of many other creatures may depend on them.'

Peter Matthiessen, *African Silences*

OPPOSITE: Elephant
engraving, Twyfelfontein.

RIGHT: Elephant traversing
basalt-strewn Damaraland.

WRITING OF HIS INFORMAL continental survey of elephant (*Loxodonta africana*) conducted in the early 1980s, author Peter Matthiessen implied that the considerable habitat requirements of these large mammals could, inadvertently, prove crucial in preserving regional biodiversity. Given the modern Western propensity for 'saving' the planet's more glamorous species, there is merit in his notion. Large tracts of land are rarely set aside for the benefit of a reptile or insect species: the traditional 'charismatic mega-fauna' are the flagships around which campaigns are fought. Indeed, the poaching epidemic of the late 1970s and early 1980s that threatened the Kunene Region's elephant and black rhinoceros populations galvanized private citizens, local residents and government officials alike to join forces to halt the butchery. Changing attitudes amongst many of the region's residents resulted in the establishment of a vanguard movement that was initially intended for the protection of high-profile animals but which, ultimately, benefited a much wider array of wildlife species. Our focus, therefore, is based on the premise that maintaining the profile of these behemoths, and promoting their conservation, will continue to have a knock-on effect, safeguarding a diverse local ecology that might otherwise be destroyed.

A family unit silently makes its way up the dry bed of the Hoarusib River. The region's elephant habitually travel considerable distances between water and their favoured feeding spots.

GARTH OWEN-SMITH

Garth Owen-Smith was the Agricultural Superintendent for the Kaokoveld from 1968 to 1970, during which time he gained an intimate knowledge of the region's people and wildlife. In his subsequent role as a conservator for the Namibia Wildlife Trust, he was instrumental in developing grassroots community involvement in an attempt to halt the plunder of the area's wildlife. He continues his active engagement with the area as co-director of Integrated Rural Development and Nature Conservation (IRDNC), a development organisation that is active in northern Namibia. Here he provides a historical narrative on the struggle of conservation officials, non-government organisations and local people in a neglected aspect of the region's recent history.

ON THE BACKGROUND TO THE POACHING . . .

Although some subsistence hunting had undoubtedly taken place, the wealthy Herero and Himba stock-owners actually looked down on hunting for meat as a socially inferior way of life. By 1977, rumours of excessive hunting of big game by high-ranking civil servants and South African Defence Force personnel had become rife. In the late seventies/early eighties, the region was struck two further blows: the worst drought on record devastated both wildlife and livestock, and SWAPO insurgents opposed to South African political domination of the territory opened a western front in Kaokoland. In order to 'protect themselves against SWAPO terrorists', the now nearly cattleless tribesmen were issued with thousands of .303 rifles. Perhaps inevitably, these guns were turned against the surviving herds of game. To make matters worse, demand for rhino horn and ivory had increased dramatically in the Middle and Far East, and their black-market value had skyrocketed.

ON THE IMPACT OF THE POACHING
ON WILDLIFE . . .

In 1977, Clive Walker of the Endangered Wildlife Trust reported that possibly fewer than 50 elephant and 15 rhino still survived in the west of the homeland. By the end of 1981, rhino and elephant had, to all intents and purposes, been wiped out in central and western Kaokoland, and well-armed gangs had started moving south into northern Damaraland. It is estimated that, by 1983, there were fewer than 300 elephant and 60 rhino left in the entire region (Kaokoland and Damaraland).

ON THE ORIGIN OF THE AUXILIARY
GAME GUARD SYSTEM . . .

In mid-1983, in conjunction with the Herero and Himba headmen in southern and western Kaokoland, and with the support of Chris Eyre (Directorate of Nature Conservation), the Namibia Wildlife Trust (NWT) started what came to be known as the auxiliary game guard programme. Under this system, area headmen selected local tribesmen and appointed them under their authority. They were supervised and given basic training by NWT and conservation officials. NWT, and later the Endangered Wildlife Trust (EWT) supplied the guards with staple rations and a small cash allowance. Although the main function of the guards was to notify the authorities of any (illegal) hunting that might take place in their areas, they were not undercover informers. Their identities were well known to the local communities. By their mere presence, the auxiliary game guards undoubtedly played a major role in deterring would-be poachers.

ON THE SIGNIFICANCE
OF THE INITIATIVE . . .

By the end of 1985 this had resulted in the conviction of over 60 people for illegal hunting. The most important contribution made by the system was the direct involvement of the local communities in the conservation of their own natural resources. Ultimately, it will be these people who decide if any game survives in the region.

(Extracted from *African Wildlife* Vol. 40 No.3, 1986.)

Lion *(Panthera leo)* spoor, Damaraland. Despite persecution from the region's livestock owners, lion continue to endure in the arid west.

THE ADVENT OF COMMUNITY-BASED CONSERVATION

Prior to the advent of formal conservation, the region's wildlife, particularly elephant, had fallen to the guns of the rapacious colonial settler era. The buoyant market for ivory, generated by consumer demand in Europe, saw 20 000 pounds of raw ivory leave the port of Walvis Bay in 1865 alone. The Angola Boers who settled the relatively verdant Angolan Highlands also hunted extensively, making regular forays into the Kaokoveld after elephant. Afrikaners made their presence felt again in the area during the period of South African rule, when misconduct (commercial and subsistence poaching – the effects of the bush war) compounded a severe local drought.

Contemporary livestock farmers have also impacted significantly on wildlife populations, particularly in the east, where boreholes and veterinary care have led to habitat deterioration as livestock numbers have increased. Predators, particularly lion and cheetah, are the major casualties of the growth of livestock farming in the region. The poisoning and hunting of 'problem animals' – predators who prey on livestock – have whittled away the already naturally low densities. There remain nucleus populations of both species in the uninhabited west, with lion continuing to roam out of the Etosha National Park, augmenting the established animals resident in this area. Although attitudes amongst many rural dwellers have changed, stock losses to predators is an emotive issue, unlikely to be tolerated, ensuring a perpetually precarious future for these two species. Leopard, jackal and the two species of hyena continue to endure largely due to their habits, and are consequently more abundant than one would expect.

OPPOSITE: A sub-adult giraffe (Giraffa camelopardalis) is an incongruous sight amongst the rugged rocks of Damaraland – a region with sparse browse resources.

ABOVE: An engraving of a giraffe, near Khowarib. Giraffe would have been a valuable prey species for the aboriginal hunter-gatherers whose legacy is evident in the beautiful engravings that litter the region's rock faces.

TJAHORERWA TJISUTA

Community Game Guard, Orupembe

Tjahorerwa Tjisuta is a member of a network of community game guards, established in the 1980s to combat a poaching epidemic provoked by the drought and brutal bush war that spilled over into northern Kaokoland. As a Himba, his primary concern is his herd of mixed livestock which he tends from his base at Orupembe, a transitory settlement at the western limit of habitable pasture. The presence of a four-wheel drive vehicle at his homestead is an incongruous sight; a recent acquisition that enables him to monitor his herds kept at outlying cattle-posts. Unable to drive himself, his eldest son is the appointed chauffeur for these excursions. There are contradictions in his dual role as farmer and custodian of the area's wildlife. Predators occasionally prey on errant goat kids and calves, the very currency he used to purchase his vehicle.

ON HIS LIFE . . .

I was born at Okatapati and grew up in this area. My father has passed away, but my mother still lives here at Orupembe. We have always farmed with our livestock, although it isn't easy to make a living. To the west is desert and there's no grass for our cattle. Nothing lives there except wildlife. One of the biggest problems we have here is the jackal, hyena and cheetah, which prey on our livestock. You can't leave animals out at night or they'll be lost to the jackal. We will remain here until the grass is finished, and then we'll have to move to the east. I don't keep all my cattle here at Orupembe, some are over the mountains to the north.

ON HIS JOB . . .

Johannes Kausana recruited me here in the presence of Garth Owen-Smith and Chris Eyre. I started the job before the bush war. I patrol the general area and keep a record of animal numbers and any that may die. It's been useful to have this work, especially during the drought, when most of my cattle died. I was left with only four cows and two bulls. I receive a small salary and some food rations every month. Because of my work there are now many animals in the area. I saw many giraffe and ostrich on my last patrol as well as springbok and zebra. The lion, rhino and elephant have all gone from this area. I remember the elephant drinking from the reservoir here at Orupembe. There were many in the area – all the way to the Kunene River. The rhino and lion are also gone, although a few years ago we saw the tracks of a lioness to the east.

ON PROGRESS AND TRADITIONS . . .

Unfortunately there aren't enough people here to have a school, so we have to send children away. Sometimes people go away to work and forget us here. One should never forget where one comes from. If someone does leave to work in the towns then they should send us something to help us. Life here is hard. We also see more tourists these days. This is a good thing if they visit us and we meet. Some don't stop and just drive by very fast. The problem is we don't know each other's cultures. Now we have a community rest-camp and can work together.

ON THE FUTURE . . .

I hope our children don't forget our ways, this is all we Himba know. Our children shouldn't forget their history and should continue to use the Holy Fire. It can help to heal and is part of our tradition. If you leave it, it can change your life.

One species that has rebounded from the depredations of the past is the elegant giraffe (*Giraffa camelopardalis*), whose numbers had come under pressure from meat poachers. They have quietly browsed their way back to a visible presence, aided by the re-introduction of animals from western Etosha. Their ability to remain independent of water, relying on the moisture content of their food, makes them a versatile resident in some remarkably difficult territory adjacent to the pro-Namib gravel plains. The favoured *Acacia*, *Combretum*, and melange of other shrubs that scatter the dry washes and valleys, sustain lone bulls and small herds. Giraffe can often be observed, bowed over, feeding on diminutive scrub, oblivious to the awkward height of their food source. In Damaraland giraffe will also ascend rocky hills in search of fresh browse – an unlikely and striking silhouette. Although they are independent of water, they will make opportunistic use of any available water source, as visual observations from the Hoanib River and the Etendeka tourist concession area confirm.

Other species that are features of the region are the hoofed legions of springbok, gemsbok and zebra that have also enjoyed the respite of the last decade. Cappuccino-brown and white springbok (*Antidorcas marsupialis*), with faces distinguished by distinct black, clownish stripes, occur throughout the North-West. Like the giraffe, they can survive without regular water, complemented by a sophisticated renal system that enables them to tolerate water with a high mineral content. Springbok are mixed feeders, preferring grass when it is available and browsing on small shrubs and bushes when it is not. Their ability to breed at any time of the year, generally synchronised with times of plenty, is a further adaptation that makes them especially suited to the demands of this inconstant habitat. Highly mobile, they migrate to favourable areas to feed, aggregating in large numbers where rainfall has created an abundance of grass.

OPPOSITE: Springbok *(Antidorcas marsupialis)* are a versatile species, able to graze and browse, shifting preference according to availability. ABOVE: Hartmann's mountain zebra (*Equus zebra hartmannae*) are a highly mobile species, inhabiting the interface between the escarpment and the western desert. This parched animal did not survive the apparent lack of graze here.

LEFT: Rain-filled dust-bath. Hartmann's mountain zebra *(Equus zebra hartmannae)* habitually roll in fine dust, creating shallow depressions that later serve as temporary waterholes after sufficient rain has fallen.

BELOW: Hartmann's mountain zebra, Damaraland. Here on the verge of the desert, this species is highly mobile, travelling up to 120 km between wet- and dry-season ranges. They also dig for water in dry rivercourses.

OPPOSITE: Gemsbok (*Oryx gazella*) drinking at a *gorra* (an excavation, often the work of elephant or even zebra, to access groundwater) against the sheer rock face backdrop of the Hoanib River.

One of the trademarks of the springbok is its bounding hop, indicating a mildly excited or agitated state, referred to as stotting or pronking. Springbok have their own particular brand of stotting. With backs bowed like cats, tails clamped, necks lowered and legs rigid like ballet dancers in mid-flight, springbok can bound as many as six times in succession. Fawns do it more often than adults, probably because they become alarmed more easily, or possibly because they are simply flexing their developing muscles.

Curious and mischievous, with an air of cavalier impudence, the Hartmann's mountain zebra (*Equus zebra hartmannae*), named after German explorer and geologist Dr Georg Hartmann, are some of the most attractive and entertaining characters of the Kunene Region. Distinguished as one of the world's rarest large mammals, they almost disappeared when the population dropped from between 50 000 to 75 000 nation-wide in the 1950s, to an estimated 5 500 in 1968. A research project established in 1969 saved these zebra from local extinction, after its recommendations resulted in their proclamation as a protected species. The population has since recovered and zebra are now a common sight north of the Ugab.

Commonly found in small groups, Hartmann's mountain zebra are unmistakably stockier than their plains cousins (*Equus burchelli*) and are characterized by a rusty tinge on the muzzle, larger ears and a small dewlap under the chin. Their stripes are also more closely set – with the shadow stripe absent – and terminate to

Ascending, spirit of the desert.

HEAT, DUST *and* **dreams**

leave a distinct white belly. They inhabit the transitional zone of mountains and grassed plains, shuttling between the two as seasonal grazing availability changes. They are impressively agile, climbing extremely steep slopes in difficult and rocky terrain to access grass and water. The zebra remain dependent on daily water – often digging in dry rivercourses to access it – and are thus vulnerable to human disturbance at springs or waterpoints.

A favourite and regular zebra pastime is dust bathing. The landscape of the North-West is riddled with large bare clearings, free of rocks, in which the zebra roll, emerging as henna-painted chargers. After rain, these depressions become temporary waterholes and are an important ancillary water source utilised by other wildlife and livestock. Their status as a subspecies, endemic to Namibia (with a possible extension in Angola's south-western mountains) entitles these zebra to high conservation priority.

An enduring, and much-touted, image of Namibia is the solitary gemsbok in an ocean of sand dunes. While perhaps less extrovert than the zebra, the gemsbok (*Oryx gazella gazella*) is entirely in its element among the dunes and aridity of the North-

Rhino tracks in the barren pro-Namib, an unlikely refuge for such a large mammal.

West. It is built like a small horse with a long, flowing tail and straight, narrow and distinctly ridged horns. With its subtle greyish bay colour and distinct black and white markings, it comes physiologically equipped to survive the thermal extremes of the desert. A unique cooling system – a series of nasal blood vessels – cools blood from the body before it reaches the brain, functioning rather like the radiator of a vehicle. This enables gemsbok to conserve water which would otherwise be expended in evaporative cooling. They also engage in various other strategies to minimise their need for moisture, including confining their movements, and feeding, to the cool of night. In addition, gemsbok are diligent in avoiding exposure to the sun and are often found resting up in shade during the midday heat.

Predominantly grazers, gemsbok also eat fruit, browse and dig for roots and tubers, enabling them to go without water for long periods. They are nomadic and sociable, generally moving in small herds, but are often found as solitary individuals. Like the springbok, they will congregate in larger groups when rains produce abundant pasture. Gemsbok will continue to find natural refuge in the arid tracts they exploit so successfully.

'I am optimistic about the future of rhino, especially in Africa . . . those to whom the grassroots responsibility has been given to protect rhino are, in my experience, as tenacious as the animals they protect'

Eugene Joubert *On the Clover Trail*, 1996

Engraving,
near Khowarib.

Black rhinoceros (*Diceros bicornis bicornis*) scrape, Western Desert.

BLACK RHINOCEROS – GREY GHOSTS OF THE DESERT

For such a large beast, the black rhinoceros is remarkably elusive. Nearly two years of fieldwork yielded no casual sightings of these animals. Evidence of their presence – dung, territorial scrape marks and their unmistakable spoor – was a reminder of what the inaccessible backcountry concealed. The fugitive habits of the Kunene rhino, and their choice of habitat, continue to offer some measure of refuge from intrusion and harassment. Regional political stability and local conservation efforts will continue to be the principal allies of the species in the region.

Myopic and curmudgeonly, the black rhinoceros, *Diceros bicornis bicornis*, serves as a reminder of a prehistoric age. A recluse of the harsh, broken country that characterises much of its habitat, its reputation of being cantankerous and unpredictable, resentful of any intrusion into its territory, is not unfounded. It has survived the threat posed by its chief adversary, man, by withdrawing to the most inaccessible and inhospitable tracts of land – and by exploiting the meagre resources available. For this reason it is recognised as a distinct subspecies.

The terrain, with its uncompromising mountain ranges and vast gravel plains, is a forbidding environment. It is dissected by innumerable rugged valleys which appear to offer limited respite to any large mammal. In spite of this, a network of natural springs enables black rhinoceros, with its diverse diet, to exploit a wide variety of browse species, including the toxic *Euphorbia virosa* and *Euphorbia damarana*, which provide some of their moisture requirements. Studies conducted to examine the feeding preferences of the species in the region show that of 103 plant species encountered, the black rhinoceros subsists comfortably on 73 of them, thus allowing them to shift preference according to availability.

Like the arid-adapted elephant of the region, the rhinoceros of the Kunene have large home ranges that vary according to the availability of water, food and cover and the number of other rhinoceros in the area. Generally, adult rhinos move throughout their range showing little concern at the presence of other animals and they appear to deal with most adversaries without much difficulty. Calves, however, are susceptible to

A rhinoceros cow and her two calves make off after smelling danger: people. The black rhinoceros has few natural enemies, its greatest threat being posed by man. One of the most critically endangered animals world-wide, it is killed for its horn. Traditional medical practitioners in the Far East and China believe it to have potent qualities and in the Middle East, and Yemen in particular, the horn is used for making dagger handles and is a status symbol.

predators and depend on their mothers for protection, remaining with them for anywhere between three and five years. Battle scars in the form of torn ears and tails are often the result of unsuccessful predator attacks.

Conservative estimates for 1960 put black rhinoceros figures in Africa at approximately 100 000. By the late 1980s more than eighty percent of these had disappeared and at the end of the 20th century this figure was as low as 2 000 animals world-wide, approximately one quarter of these in Namibia. The Kunene region, covering an estimated 25 000 square kilometres, is currently home to roughly one third of Namibia's black rhinoceros population. It is interesting that the majority of these animals roam communal land with no formal protection.

Prior to 1966 most of Namibia's black rhinoceros were to be found outside of protected areas. In an effort to offer better protection to the species, a major translocation programme was initiated ensuring that seventy percent were within protected areas by the late 1970s. Some 43 rhino were translocated from Damaraland to Etosha National Park, leaving relict populations of approximately 100 and 150 in Damaraland and Kaokoland respectively. However, the late 1970s and early 1980s saw a massive upsurge in the number of animals killed by poachers, some of whom were SADF military staff and local residents. The result was that in 1982, the estimated number of black rhinoceros surviving in the region was as low as 40. In an effort to put a stop to the rampant poaching, local people were recruited in a pilot scheme that was to be the forerunner of future community-based conservation initiatives: the auxiliary game guard programme was set up for the sole purpose of monitoring and protecting wildlife.

'The Rhino Arms', Rooivlak.

Rhino art, Save the Rhino Trust camp, Ugab River.

BLYTHE LOUTIT

Founding Member and Director, Save the Rhino Trust (SRT)

Having teetered on the brink of extinction, the black rhinoceros appears to be experiencing a reprise in the region. This is largely due to the efforts and determination of the Ministry of Environment and Tourism (MET), the Community Game Guard Programme and Save the Rhino Trust (SRT), who have acted as vanguards in the race to halt the local extinction of the species. SRT was set up in an effort

to halt the upsurge in poaching which the region experienced in the seventies and eighties. Since its inception, the Trust has collaborated with Government and local communities to provide security for the rhino, monitor the rhino population in the region, and bring benefit to the community through conservation and tourism.

During its infancy, the Trust employed convicted poachers because of their extensive knowledge of rhinoceros habits. Along with trackers from the Community Game Guard Programme, patrols of the territory were initiated to provide an extensive and comprehensive system of information and guardianship for all threatened mammals in the territory. Working in co-operation with MET, the community and other non-government organisations (NGOs), a full census of the rhino population is undertaken by SRT every five years. Figures show that the black rhino population in the North-West has all but doubled since the formation of the Trust and that poaching has declined exponentially.

Blythe Loutit being a founding member, her name is now synonymous with the welfare of rhinoceros. The genial Loutit is a determined and formidable champion for a cause that has, at times, seemed hopeless. She divides her time between her home in Swakopmund and the network of SRT base camps in the Kunene.

ON HOW IT ALL STARTED . .

In the early 1980s, a savage slaughter of desert wildlife was taking place. As the rhino numbers shrank to near extinction, a group of concerned people gathered together to form a trust fund. Our aim was to stop the horrendous slaughter of rhino, elephant and other wildlife that was taking place in the desert – killing that was being perpetrated by military staff of the SADF and white government officials who paid subsistence farmers to hunt the more inaccessible rhino. With the hard work and dedication of these founding members, including the community, and the financial help of international donors, the Save the Rhino Trust was born and officially recognised and registered as a charitable organisation. Since that time poaching has drastically declined and the rhino population has more than doubled.

ON TURNING THE SITUATION AROUND . . .

There was a time, when poaching was at its height, that we thought we would never be able to overcome the problem. It seemed so out of hand in the beginning, but it has been a great surprise to achieve the success that we have.

ON OPERATION BICORNIS, THE DEHORNING PROGRAMME OF THE LATE EIGHTIES . . .

The dehorning programme in the North-West was instigated because of an upsurge in poaching in the late 1980s/early 1990s. The then government and SRT decided that in order to safeguard the region's rhino population, drastic measures had to be taken. Poaching had claimed seven rhino and we had received information that there were plans to kill more. Our funds at that time were insufficient to cope with patrolling the huge area in question so, in order to save the rhino, we went ahead with the dehorning programme. Although there were many opponents to the programme, those animals that were dehorned have, contrary to some expectations, survived in a normal manner. Relatively few rhino were dehorned and it is unlikely that the programme will be repeated since there are now sufficient funds and people working in the field to patrol the area.

ON THE SUSTAINABLE USE OF RHINO . . .

I believe that sustainable use can best be achieved through the dehorning and farming of rhino horn. I am not a great supporter of one individual benefiting from the horn, as with trophy hunting. Greater attention should be paid to the increasing use of rhino horn in the traditional Asian medicines. Trade is increasing worldwide, and emerging Asian centres, for example Chinatown in Montreal, are witnessing an increase in the use of animal parts for traditional medicine. If horn were farmed, then there would be less (illegal) killing of rhino in the wild. Farming the horn is one way of utilising wildlife without killing it.

ON CONSERVANCIES . . .

The ideal behind the development of a conservancy is great! Unfortunately for communities however, the ideal has brought huge expectations. Conservancies were created in Natal in the early 1970s to protect fauna and flora in areas where farm boundaries cut through natural ecosystems, or where ranchers wanted to allow wildlife larger home ranges. The system works well for them. But they are wealthy people – private farmers and businessmen – and they have the resources to implement and maintain the programme. They draw up agreements with the Parks Board, and employ their own game guards from the local community, providing them with vehicles and fuel. For many of these ranchers the aim is altruistic – they are not seeking to make a profit from the conservancies. The system of communal conservancies, on the other hand, seeks to financially benefit the communities. It is an ideal that will always need external funding to exist. Sadly, conservancies in communal areas feature small-scale, land-grabbing disputes dominated by stronger members of the community, leaving the more timid sector unable to feature in the development process. This has also caused unnecessary conflict between communal ethnic groups. The conservancy system in arid western Namibia does not work well for the rhino, elephant and most wildlife, which moves in and out of a conservancy boundary. A biosphere park or multi-use area would be well suited to communal areas and could incorporate conservancies as well.

ON THE WAY FORWARD . . .

SRT is working with local communities and with the Ministry's Rhino Advisory Committee on a comprehensive Rhino Management Plan for communal areas. It has always been my hope that SRT be fully integrated in any future plan for conservation in communal areas. With the Minister of Environment's announcement that there will be a proclamation for wildlife in this area, SRT can make considerable contributions to a conservation system for these areas. As an organisation, we are hoping to reduce many of our activities to concentrate on training and information publications that will help develop the capacity of local people in conservation and tourism. At the moment, SRT run basic ecology and hospitality training courses. In addition, we plan to run basic tourism courses with trainers who are familiar with the area and the people. Our strategy is to continue working closely with traditional leaders and the local communities.

ON THE FUTURE OF THE BLACK RHINO IN NAMIBIA . . .

Rhino in the desert have a very good future, and it is time to sell some rhino to set up breeding groups outside of Namibia, so that we can show the community the true value of live rhino.

NAMIBIA
N$ 5.00

NAM POST 3.8 **Black Rhino**

Credit/Acknowledgements: © NAMPOST Artist: Helge Denker

UGAB RIVER
SAVE THE RHINO TRUST BASE CAMP

The Ugab River Campsite was built in January 1997 with some local materials, a small amount of money and a lot of hard work. It serves the dual purpose of being both a base camp for Save the RhinoTrust rhino patrols, and for providing a comfortable campsite for tourists passing through the area. All money donated by tourists goes directly to the local people who look after and run the camp and craft shop

If you would like to participate in a rhino monitoring trip, simply talk to one of the camp staff. It will give you the chance to view this spectacular landscape and see its wildlife, including the rare black desert rhino, with a guide who knows the area well. There is the same variety of wildlife that can be seen in game parks - zebra, giraffe, oryx, elephant, rhino ~ just in a larger area!

kudu
jackal
oryx
zebra
rhino

© SRT

MANNETJIE GANASEB

Project Manager of the Camel Patrol, Save the Rhino Trust

Before following a career as one of the pioneering auxiliary game guards, Joel Ganaseb spent his early working life hunting the wildlife of the Kunene to feed his family. His son Mannetjie now patrols the very same territory: the hostile lava desert south of the Hoanib River.

Based at Khowarib, Mannetjie followed his father into conservation and considers the rhino he monitors to be as valuable as his own livestock, a telling notion in a region where cattle, goats and sheep are revered. Mannetjie leads camel patrols that are conducted to monitor the status of rhino in the area. He also photographs the animals for the SRT database – a record of the life history of all the Kunene rhino – and is renowned for getting rather close to his unpredictable subjects.

ON HIS BACKGROUND . . .

I am Damara – we are ten children in our family, three boys and seven girls – and grew up here in Khowarib. I'm married with six children and joined SRT in 1986 as a junior tracker. I'm now a senior tracker responsible for the camel patrol.

ON HIS JOB . . .

I learnt about the bush and animals by spending time hunting as a boy with my father. There were no jobs at that time and my father had no other choice but to hunt for meat to feed his family. We used to hunt using dogs, with donkeys for transport. We only hunted antelope, not the elephant or rhino. My father later became a game guard, and I, in turn, have followed him into a job in the bush. We normally have seven days off a month, the rest are spent on patrol. We check the health of rhino, and if there have been any calves born. We don't use maps – our heads are our maps. People in my community have asked me how I can be away from home for so long with my job. It's quite simple: this job enables me to support my family. Many people in this area have no job at all.

M Ganaseb © SRT

M Ganaseb © SRT

ON RHINO . . .

Rhino are like my cattle. I know them very well. I can recognise all the rhino in my area. In 1997 I was shown how to use a camera and I've been taking pictures of the rhino since then. I like to get really close for my pictures. Each rhino has a name with a file at our office. We usually name a newborn calf after someone from the group that first sights the animal. There's a rhino named after me. Mrs Blythe (SRT Director) was with us when we discovered this calf and decided that its name would be Mannetjie. Rhino can be dangerous if you are inexperienced. You have to be careful tracking them. You should never run if a rhino approaches and if it does, you should move back slowly, one step at a time. A rhino isn't as mobile as an elephant so you usually have time to move out of the way if it charges. They have a very good sense of smell, and if you smoke (tobacco) they might come to investigate – that's happened to me. Some people in these areas would love to get hold of rhino horn to sell. However, it's impossible for anyone to poach here because SRT and the community game guards patrol all over. A patrol might be behind this mountain right now with their donkeys. Access is also very difficult for strangers to the area. The local community will immediately report anything suspicious. In the 1980s a lot of rhino and elephant were shot in this area. We arrested some of the people after receiving local information. They'd been working for people from outside.

ON CAMELS . . .

We've used camels for a few years now. I'm in charge of the camel patrol team. We attended a six-month course in Swakopmund on how to handle and care for them. Camels are perfect for our kind of work, and are stronger than donkeys. We don't ride them, but they carry our supplies.

We also carry food for them so they stay strong. They've adapted well to the area and aren't afraid of any of the wildlife we see. I've seen them eat most of the vegetation except for the milk bush (Euphorbia damarana). It's poisonous. They don't need to drink water often and can go where vehicles can't. The hump on their back is like an extra water tank.

M Ganaseb © SRT

THE DESERT ELEPHANT ENIGMA

Interest in the remote reaches of the Kunene Region has grown exponentially since Namibian independence. While some visitors are attracted by cultural elements, or by the region's grand landscapes, the majority make the pilgrimage in search of a particular animal: the elephant. Those beasts inhabiting the western extent of the region, which rarely receives more than 150 mm of rainfall per annum, have been propelled into the public consciousness as the near mythical 'desert elephant'.

Hyperbole dominates popular perception of these enigmatic behemoths and images of them improbably negotiating sand dunes – a fanciful vision of a Saharan spectacle where pachyderms replace

OPPOSITE: Bull elephant at rest, Hoanib River. ABOVE: Dwarfed by the steep mountains that mark the passage of the Hoanib River, a bull elephant makes for midday shade.

A breeding herd on the move in Damaraland, using the region's dry riverbeds to navigate their rock-strewn habitat. This herd has just indulged in a rare mud-bath, and have taken on the rusty-red colour of the soil substrate.

Elephant have been propelled into the public consciousness as the near-mythical 'desert elephant'.

An elephant drinking at a *gorra* gives an immediate sense of the scale of the Hoanib River.

camels – have endowed them with considerable aura. Visitors are thus often rather disappointed to find the animals feeding amongst a verdant Mediterranean backdrop of wild tamarisk (*Tamarix usneoides*) brush in the Hoarusib River, or slumbering under the broad boughs of an ana tree (*Faidherbia albida*) in the Ugab River. Reality is, inevitably, somewhat less melodramatic.

The rationale for their presence in this marginal and precarious habitat is uncertain. As in other parts of the continent, loss of habitat and the attentions of man have certainly affected their local range. Although these animals do inhabit a hyper-arid environment, the majority of their lives is spent in, or near, the seasonal rivers that course westward. The vegetated lifelines that are the ephemeral rivers, characterised by a savanna complex of riverine trees and shrubs, penetrate deep into the pro-Namib. Apart from providing the substantial dietary requirements of the elephant, these seasonal rivers are a fund of precious groundwater, appearing as springs and wetlands in the rivercourses. The elephant confine themselves to these meridians for most of the year, venturing further afield if rain provides a springboard to explore the hinterland. Without this confined, but generous habitat, it is unlikely that these huge beasts could survive on the saline springs and desiccated shrubs that distinguish the bulk of the region.

Another questionable myth surrounds their supposed frugal feeding behaviour, whereby they refrain from destroying vegetation in the course of their daily activities. Opponents of the 'responsible feeding' theory argue that this is a reflection of generally low elephant densities in the region. They support this argument with data from the Hoanib River, which indicates significant impact of elephant feeding behaviour on ana trees in particular.

Research into the habitat preference of elephant lists rivers and the associated floodplains as their most-favoured haunts. Sand dunes, unsurprisingly, earn least-favoured habitat status. Images of elephant cresting sand dunes are therefore likely to involve animals in transit or on a brief seasonal reconnaissance.

This is not to detract from their ability to endure, and indeed flourish, in this drought-prone environment. No desert-dwelling elephant were recorded to have died as a direct result of the crippling 1977–1982 drought. Mortalities amongst other arid-adapted mammals, such as springbok (*Antidorcas marsupialis*) and gemsbok (*Oryx gazella gazella*) were significant. In addition, during this period, the elephant showed no desire to migrate towards the east where conditions were less severe. The elephant's apparent resilience can be attributed to a number of factors, including a catholic diet and a high degree of mobility that permits them to travel up to 70 kilometres in a 24-hour period. This enables utilisation of food resources at a greater distance from a water source. The relatively sparse distribution of food resources, coupled with the distance they must commute to water, translates into larger home ranges than those recorded for other elephant populations on the continent.

With their distinct height advantage, they are able to access vegetation – such as the towering ana trees that grace the seasonal rivers – that is beyond the reach of most other animals. They can also delay drinking for up to four days and can access underground water by digging in sandy riverbeds. However, all this is underlined by the inherent knowledge, amongst mature animals, of the location of resources within their individual ranges. This enables groups with calves to negotiate the formidable 70 kilometres of aridity that lies between the Hoanib and Hoarusib Rivers, a journey made regularly by certain

GORRAS

THE ART OF SOURCING WATER IS A SKILL of immeasurable importance for the elephant of this arid quarter, which depend on a network of scattered springs to sustain them for the majority of the year. These animals are also accomplished 'water-diviners', digging for groundwater in the sandy riverbeds to supplement the precious oases. The resulting excavations, known locally by the Damara term *'gorras'*, provide a source of clean, cool water, demonstrating the elephants' preference for uncontaminated, subterranean water – an inclination that may not be solely based on whim. Research in Botswana and Zimbabwe has recorded drought-related elephant mortalities caused by the consumption of highly saline water.

Digging a *gorra* requires equanimity and a refined sense of smell. These excavations are commonly sited to exploit the presence of shallow groundwater, forced to the surface by impermeable bedrock, and are apparently revisited, and re-excavated, on an annual basis. Adult elephant of both sexes excavate *gorras*, with younger animals often becoming restless at the deliberate patience the process requires. The front feet are initially used to scoop out the surface sand, with the trunk employed to clear the hole of the later muddy seepage. If the *gorra* has already been utilised by an earlier visitor, it is usually cleaned prior to re-use. While the sand-filtered water seeps slowly up to the surface, the attendant animals stand calmly by. Patience is the ultimate virtue in this exercise, with the rewards evidently significant enough to warrant the extra effort.

There is a whole series of *gorras* in the Hoanib River, regularly favoured over a natural, saline, spring in the vicinity. There would appear to be a pattern of seasonal utilisation of these *gorras* by the resident elephant, which may correlate to the level of the fluctuating water table. This level is governed

by the amount of recharge received by the groundwater store during a given season. With the onset of the dry season the water table drops as evaporation increases, raising the salinity of the soil and water at the spring. Observation of increased elephant activity at the *gorras*, coinciding with the advancement of the dry season, highlights the value of this alternative subterranean source.

Access to the *gorras*, particularly in remote locales, benefits a whole range of other mammals, birds and insects unable to dig for themselves. Gemsbok, baboon, jackal and leopard are some of the larger mammals that profit from the efforts of elephant in the Hoanib River. Early travellers to the sub-region also found these diggings a useful water source whilst traversing arid tracts, using them to replenish their own supplies and to water livestock. The Himba continue to create similar, albeit deeper, natural wells in the region's sand rivers to water their livestock, as well as to sustain themselves.

A matriarch patiently excavates a gorra in the bed of the Hoanib River.

individual animals and family units. These elephant habitually abandon their established dry season ranges after significant rain, when standing water enables them to exploit the hinterland to indulge their appetites for fresh forbs and new shoots.

Whilst these elephant are popularly assigned the 'desert elephant' label, there are two other distinct populations in the region, each inhabiting its own, equally austere, geographical range. One group inhabits the fringe of the Great Escarpment west of Etosha, migrating to and from Etosha National Park and the former Ovamboland and, increasingly, venturing onto the farms of the Outjo district. Another grouping is centred in and around the rugged Grootberg Mountains. These animals make infrequent contact with both other populations, and range westward to the myriad of springs that fringe the pro-Namib, formidable terrain with little shelter in the form of large trees. Nor are they averse to climbing the precipitous inselbergs of Damaraland in search of food in the form of new growth, a sight not uncommon during the wet season.

Despite their public profile, much remains unknown about the elephant of the Kunene Region. This paucity of data is particularly relevant given the current advent of controlled hunting in the area, promoted via the conservancy initiative. Insights into the long-term movement of elephant, their social organisation and population structure will validate a coherent management strategy for the species. The historical persecution that has blighted our relationship with these magnificent beasts would suggest circumspection in determining this future.

THE CONSERVATION ETHIC

Rekindling a wildlife conservation ethic among the people of the region, a feat of considerable diplomacy, is largely responsible for the resurgence in wildlife numbers in many parts of the Kunene Region. The initiative of the early pioneers of community-based conservation and their disciples, some of whom are profiled in this work, must be acknowledged. Their vision, a synthesis of people and wildlife, is the bedrock for a secure future for all stakeholders. Wildlife is an increasingly integral part of the economic future of the region's people. The profits generated by visitors, yearning to view or hunt an elephant or springbok, may ultimately ensure their survival.

Two bulls meet to feed on the expansive Hoanib River floodplain, Skeleton Coast Park, with the northern dune field as a backdrop. The floodplain is a popular post-flood feeding area.

the way forward

harnessing the region's potential

'Knowledge itself

is power . . .'

Francis Bacon (1561-1626)
Meditations Sacrae (1597)

OPPOSITE: A water supply fortified
against the sometimes destructive
attentions of thirsty elephant.

RIGHT: Wind provides the power
to pump water into small reservoirs.

LIVING WITH BEHEMOTHS

The Kunene is a dry, thirsty place with sparsely distributed springs and waterpoints, a scarce resource shared between people and wildlife. No animal is thirstier than the elephant that lumber out of the parched desert to frequent borehole troughs and reservoirs. To local residents they can prove to be a malevolent and destructive presence, exacerbating an already precarious existence. The dichotomy between this reality and the position elephant occupy in popular Western culture is especially acute. Rural dwellers are often unable to comprehend the allure of these potentially dangerous beasts to visitors desperate to view and photograph them.

With the majority of wildlife in Namibia found outside of protected areas, the potentially destructive power of wildlife is a vivid reality for rural people. Elephant are responsible for considerable damage as they raid vegetable gardens, damage waterpoints and kill livestock. Occasionally the necessity of sharing waterpoints and living space leads to tragic consequences for local residents as they go about their daily chores. Post-independence Namibia has seen a decline in human pressure (illegal hunting) on elephant. In the Kunene Region, the robust elephant population roams communal land at will and is not confined to the often-protective cocoon of a game reserve or national park. This has allowed them to expand into once-familiar territory. They have, for example, successfully recolonised portions of the Ugab River, an area from which they had been absent for close on four decades.

In the shadow of Brandberg Mountain the Ugab elephant have made a habit of frequenting the Nunues family dwelling. Although she had been living there for five years, Elizabeth Nunues had never seen an elephant until 1998. In the absence of her husband, a migrant

ABOVE: Measures to create defences around water supplies include surrounding the source with rocks or modifying the construction so that elephant can also access the water without destroying the precious machinery

OPPOSITE, TOP: Elizabeth Nunues milking her goats..

OPPOSITE, BOTTOM: Elephant occasionally visit Etendeka Mountain Camp, a reminder that wildlife is never very far away.

mineworker, she tends approximately one hundred goats and sheep, selling milk locally to make ends meet. The makeshift wire fence surrounding the vegetable patch is frequently brushed aside as the elephant sate their appetite for the forbidden fruit and vegetables. The water trough is often drained, leaving her flock waterless, particularly if a wind does not rise to turn the windmill. Nights spent restraining the dogs and cowering in her fragile home have not endeared the beasts to Elizabeth Nunues.

At De Riet, west of Khorixas, there is, however, cause for optimism. Here a pragmatic synergy exists between the thirsty giants and the handful of local farmers. Cattle and goats remain corralled until mid-morning whilst three dusty elephant bulls draw trunkfulls of water from the reservoir. Only after the elephant move off to rest in nearby shade does the farmer release his livestock to drink. The elephant do not arrive at the same time every day, often drinking in the cool calm of night. Nonetheless, it is a remarkable display of tolerance. In another reasoned approach – the consequence of a collaborative initiative involving the local conservancy, non-government bodies and conservation officials – farmers build battlements of rock encircling windmills and waterpoints to keep elephant from vandalising costly pipes and pumps. Some have been constructed to allow the elephant limited access to the reservoir. With livestock husbandry the backbone of most communal area residents' livelihoods, expecting them to withstand the persistent distress caused by wildlife is unreasonable and shortsighted. It is likely, therefore, that the expanding elephant population of Kunene will, increasingly, require similar philanthropic initiatives from local residents.

ECO-TOURISM: FACT OR FALLACY?

'Those who would prefer their landscapes unspoiled – as I do – should consider whether they want other people's human potential to be trapped forever within the simple life, for the sake of the tourist's patronage.'

Nuala O'Faolain (1998)

Thoughtless drivers leave their mark on this delicate landscape. Slow-growing lichens, which inhabit the Namib coast, are the primary victims in this case.

DUNCAN GILCHRIST
Guide and raconteur, Kamanjab

Kamanjab is where the tar road ends and the network of dirt tracks that serves the wilderness of the far north begins. This often bustling frontier town boasts two supermarkets, a filling station, a guest house and . . . Duncan Gilchrist. Gilchrist runs his own safari operation from the well-stocked Poor Boys Bottle Store in Kamanjab. With a reputation for enjoying life, Gilchrist's encyclopaedic knowledge of the Kunene Region is legendary, albeit as an addendum to his extra-curricular exploits. He is the archetypal conservator-turned-guide, choosing tourism over the bureaucracy and politics of the formal conservation world. In conversation, he reveals a deep empathy with the wildlife and people of the Kunene. Although he hails from Dumbartonshire in Scotland, he is perhaps more of an African than many others conceived on these shores, and an unassuming and articulate one at that.

ON THE EARLY DAYS . . .

I worked for a hunter before moving into conservation. We built Palmwag as a hunting camp. I then worked for the Directorate of Nature Conservation from 1983 until 1994, based at Otjivasandu in Etosha and later Sesfontein. This was the time when poaching in the region intensified dramatically with the bush war moving into Kaokoland. The poachers moved south as the bush war escalated. My colleague, Chris Eyre, and I decided we had to do something before Damaraland's wildlife was slaughtered. Using local informants and regular patrols we began to make an impact. The army (South African Defence Force) was also guilty of poaching. Kaokoland was a huge hunting concession for the top brass. Koevoet (South African Police Counter-Insurgency Unit) didn't give a damn either. Those were the best years of my life. Now there are too many competing personalities and egos, particularly in the NGO field. They often end up doing the same things, duplicating the work.

ON TOURISM . . .

There is no place in Africa like the Kaokoland. It is like a huge playground with no rules. Where else can you camp, drive – basically do what you want – in amongst desert elephant, rhino, lion, and all this amazing scenery? We used to think that there were too many people in the Hoanib during the bush war, when the army was patrolling the river. Now it's totally out of control with all the self-drive tourists. It's too easy to blame South African visitors for all the abuses; but local Namibians are also to blame, including our tour operators and their guides.

ON ELEPHANT . . .

The elephant were skittish in the 1980s when all the poaching was going on. They used to move off at speed when they saw a car. However, they have calmed down a lot since then – and their numbers have increased.

But now with all the tourist traffic in the rivers they're getting hassled by people again. The rivers are where the shade and food are – there's no other suitable habitat. People have this image of the 'desert elephant'. They want to keep this myth alive, and so they harass the elephant out of the riverbeds in order to get the coveted photo with a sand dune as backdrop.

Then there are the movie crews that camp near the springs and follow the elephant for weeks on end.

ON CONSERVANCIES . . .

The conservancies here are too money-oriented and have been given false hope by Zimbabwe's CAMPFIRE model. In Zimbabwe, impala are like goats and there are even too many elephant in some areas. This region is nothing like that. There aren't enough animals here to generate that sort of income from hunting. Also, conservancies have no legal jurisdiction over access to areas, so it's difficult for them to control tourism from that point of view.

I favour a contractual national park, where the state is the policeman, but where local people still have access to the protected area – such as for grazing. This model was proposed in the eighties for the area west of the Kaokoveld, with full approval from the local people, but nothing came of it.

ABOVE AND BELOW: Boni Awarab, consummate guide, runs through the itinerary before taking his guests for a walk. Guided walks and drives are a valuable introduction to the subtle features of the Etendeka Concession.

Post-independence Namibia is an increasingly popular destination for tourists, with the travel industry generating significant revenue and employment. A concerted effort by the national tourist authority to sell Namibia abroad as a unique and untamed destination has seen a considerable increase in the number of 'self-drive' tourists, as well as large groups of budget travellers, in search of 'wilderness' and 'adventure'. Since 1990 the Kunene Region has also seen a marked growth in the number of visitors, although given the size of the territory, the figures still remain relatively low. General infrastructure, specifically roads, is poor with only the more determined – or wealthy – visitor able to access the remote reaches of the region. In an area with marginal agricultural potential, local inhabitants rely on tending livestock and on subsistence cultivation. With high unemployment, further exacerbated by a local population growth estimated at 4% per annum, tourism offers the residents of the Kunene Region a rare opportunity to engage in the formal economy – a potential lifeline for those who struggle to make ends meet.

There are some, though, who view the advent of mass tourism as the death knell for this fragile wilderness. In spite of the relatively low numbers of visitors, the inevitable debris of tourism is increasingly discernible. Growing numbers of off-road safaris entice visitors into these 'unspoilt' reaches, previously accessible only to local pastoralists. This is manifest in the innumerable vehicle tracks that scar the Namib's lichen fields and other ecologically sensitive areas. Added to this are the more subtle impacts of disruption and harassment that vehicle convoys cause to wildlife, particularly in the narrow confines of the river valleys.

The Skeleton Coast Camp, run by Wilderness Safaris, is an exercise in 'luxury' eco-tourism. Nestling unobtrusively among the dunes, the *en suite* tents provide an unexpected level of comfort. The ethos is to have as little impact on this fragile environment as possible. Solar power is the order of the day. Water and wood are carried in from outside the concession and water utilisation is carefully monitored. Guests are encouraged to utilise these resources wisely.

With high unemployment, tourism offers the residents of the Kunene Region

a rare opportunity to engage in the formal economy. There are a number of

community-run campsites in the region: Nganga Camp (LEFT); Khowarib

Community Campsite (BELOW); and SRT Ugab River Campsite (OPPOSITE).

the Himba, priceless family heirlooms are all too often sold for distressingly low figures. There is also a worrying increase in begging or expecting something for nothing: adults soliciting tobacco, children demanding sweets at every opportunity. The consequences of having no formal control over the number, or behaviour, of tourists entering these fragile areas are increasingly evident.

A growing number of concession holders are striving to run their operations with as little impact on the environment as possible. By building, and running, camps in a truly eco-friendly manner (monitoring water usage, importing firewood from outside the concession, employing members of the local community), they are actively involved in safeguarding the region for the future. From the luxury Skeleton Coast Camp run by Wilderness Safaris, to the privately owned Etendeka Mountain Camp, overseas visitors are encouraged to take stock of, and appreciate, the fragile environment and its limited resources.

While most tour operators and self-drive overseas visitors generally behave in a responsible fashion, many local visitors (Namibian and South African) view the region with a certain amount of possessive disregard. For them, the Kunene Region is 'their last wilderness' – 'their' being the operative word – and they consider it a constitutional right to camp and drive wherever they choose. Visitors are also increasingly impacting on local culture. Eager to possess tangible proof of their brush with the 'authentic' and 'traditional' culture of

DENNIS LIEBENBERG
Etendeka Mountain Camp

Etendeka could easily pass for a prototype Mars base camp, a cluster of canvas amongst the lunar landscape of the rugged Grootberg Mountains. Owner Dennis Liebenberg has created a solar-powered refuge that offers few of the trappings that the plethora of 'boutique' lodges flaunt. A strictly 'no frills' approach is taken to furnishings and décor, reminiscent of a

hunters' camp. Here the emphasis is on walking trails that focus on the area's geology and arid-adapted flora. Liebenberg has also taken a pro-active approach with regard to community responsibility, instituting a bed-night levy that has ploughed over N$70 000 into communal coffers since 1995.

ON GETTING ETENDEKA STARTED . . .

The camp has evolved over ten years. We started out catering for camping groups who slept on camp stretchers in small dome tents. I remember setting up the camp with a pride of lions in attendance! Extremes of temperature, high winds and precipitation are the most difficult to endure. Access is difficult, the terrain is extremely rugged and is very hard on vehicles, but this is a small price to pay for the true wilderness experience we offer here.

ON ALTERNATIVE ENERGY . . .

Namibia is really the perfect location for making use of alternative energy sources. We rely on the energy that two banks of solar panels convert to keep a system of long-life batteries charged. This runs our low-voltage fridges, freezers, communications and lighting requirements. Solar power is an attractive option for my operation, as it doesn't generate noise or pollution. It is also safe and requires very little maintenance. Unfortunately, it's still an expensive technology to acquire; otherwise it would be more widely exploited here. We also use solar water heaters, which are extremely efficient. Water is our major limiting factor and we ask guests to use it sparingly. The use of simple bucket showers and low-flush toilets keeps our water consumption down to as little as 60 litres per person per day.

ON COMMUNITY-BASED TOURISM . . .

I was very fortunate to find a well-established system of community-based conservation when I started here. I've always advocated the involvement of local communities in conservation and tourism. As far as I'm concerned, this is the only way forward for the industry in this region. We instituted a voluntary bed-night levy that raised money for local communities. It's essential for such benefits to be realised by local communities if they're going to have an interest in conservation and a positive perception of tourism initiatives.

ON WILDLIFE VERSUS CATTLE . . .

This area is utilised by semi-nomadic people with goats and sheep and is, in my opinion, a marginal area for livestock, particularly cattle. Cattle are limited by their reliance on water, which limits their mobility considerably, and can lead to overgrazing. The sporadic rainfall we get here is exploited by wildlife species such as springbok, oryx and mountain zebra. Because of their increased mobility over domestic stock they often share the same water sources as the goats but are able to move further to graze. If it rains to the west, the game moves off within a few days.

ON THE FUTURE . . .

The tourist concession that I have will be incorporated into a conservancy in the near future. Conservancy legislation allows operators like me to negotiate contracts directly with local communities, so much greater benefits can flow directly to local people at grassroots level. I feel that this is the start of the payback to local people for twenty years of community-based conservation.

The danger that lies ahead is one of ill-planned and uncontrolled development: after all, the product we sell is pristine wilderness in all its unpopulated splendour.

MONICA USES
Entrepreneur, Khowarib

Monica is the driving force behind the Anmire Cultural Village, based at the small settlement of Khowarib on the banks of the Hoanib River. Monica got her idea for a Damara traditional village after a visit to a similar venture in the Caprivi. Prior to this, she had sold curios at a small roadside stall to support her three children. She mobilised the local residents and built the model village at the foot of the impressive canyon that dwarfs the settlement.

ON DAMARA CULTURE . . .

We are a very diverse people. Damara have always lived with the land. Some Damara originate from the coast, where they survived collecting nara *(melon) and fish, but my family came from the Brandberg area. Damara traditions are disappearing: our children aren't familiar with or, apparently, interested in most of them. Even I had to visit the village elders to find out about the old stories and ways. But it's beginning to change and people in the village can now see the value of our work and are glad that we're reviving and preserving the Damara culture.*

We show visitors all aspects of our culture: fire making, traditional dances and how our traditional houses developed from basic rock to pole and plaster structures.

ON GETTING STARTED . . .

We obtained a loan in 1997 to start the traditional village and we've had a lot of support from IRDNC who have been wonderful. I've also attended several training courses on working with tourists, sponsored by NACOBTA. We started out with too many staff, and we couldn't pay all the salaries, so there are only three staff now. Our main problem is that there aren't many visitors in the summer months, so we don't generate much income.

ON THE FUTURE . . .

We definitely need more visitors to make Anmire profitable. It's hard seeing tourists driving past without stopping. It would be nice to be able to give something back to the community.

Non-governmental organisations – key players

In an effort to augment already limited incomes, and in response to the increased numbers of visitors to the region, local communities and individuals have established a variety of rustic campsites. Whilst they filled an unexploited niche, many of the ventures have been beset by teething problems. With little or no experience in this service industry, and often constrained by a lack of capital, many provide indifferent services and facilities. For some, community-based tourism is a vehicle that attracts significant amounts of donor funding and, as such, is open to exploitation: everybody wants a piece of the pie. In an attempt to reverse this trend, two non-governmental organisations, the Namibian Community-Based Tourism Association (NACOBTA) and Integrated Rural Development and Nature Conservation (IRDNC), have become key players in assisting the emerging tourist sector.

Inaugurated in 1995, NACOBTA boasts involvement in more than 40 established and emerging projects. The aim of the organisation is to support and enable predominantly rural communities to benefit directly from their cultural and natural resources by engaging in tourism ventures. Based on the underlying premise of sustainable and responsible use of those resources, the objective is to encourage economic and social empowerment in previously disadvantaged communities. By increasing employment opportunities and generating income, communities are encouraged to be responsible guardians and to recognise the value of their resources. Projects include running training courses and providing advice and logistical support for setting up community-run campsites, rest camps, traditional villages, local tour-guide facilities, tourist information centres and communal area conservancies. IRDNC concerns itself more with responsible utilisa-

Conservancies are being formed all over the North-West.

CONSERVANCIES – A SYNTHESIS OF WILDLIFE AND PEOPLE?

The shift toward an inclusivist approach to natural resource management is a relatively recent phenomenon in Africa. Colonial attitudes of subjugating and demarcating nature in the form of reserves created islands of no-go areas with fences, signposts and epauletted officials that turned local communities into poachers – trespassers on land that had sustained their very existence. This only served to alienate rural dwellers from the 'conservation' cause. Dispossession has come full circle with the current focus on managing environments holistically. Programmes now aim to address the needs of wildlife and people. Conservation has also evolved a fiscal face that seeks to incorporate rural development in its agenda. Assigning value to wildlife, determined on the basis of how much revenue tourists, or hunters, can contribute to the local economy, is intended to safeguard against unsustainable exploitation of this resource.

Namibian Conservancy Programme

The Namibian Conservancy Programme is, in essence, a hybrid of various programmes already in existence on the sub-continent – a partnership between government, non-government and local institutions. This particular evolution is significant as it has seen legislation grant communal area residents user rights over wildlife, a privilege to which commercial farmers have had access for over thirty years. Prior to this, wildlife numbers on private farms were extremely low, but the introduction of user rights saw a huge increase in wildlife and tourism. The programme is a major departure from previous incarnations of community-based projects, which have often been executed or managed via an arm of the state. The project with the highest profile in

tion of natural resources, primarily wildlife. One of its chief roles is as an intermediary between communities and the private sector – a relationship seen as a blueprint for the future of the industry in the region. It is also facilitating the implementation of the conservancy initiative.

There is little doubt that tourism will continue to feature as a growth industry in the North-West. As the conservancy ethos strengthens its grip, rural stakeholders will increasingly look to tourist-based ventures as potentially lucrative undertakings. The challenge of harnessing this potential will fall to the emerging conservancies and their new partners in the private sector.

the sub-region, if not the continent, is the CAMPFIRE programme (Communal Areas Management Programme for Indigenous Resources) in Zimbabwe. Initiated in the early 1980s, popularly elected Regional District Councils are state structures that act as conduits for a number of local community structures to manage their natural resources.

Local conservancies are formed via a consultative process that requires the community to meet certain preconditions before submitting their application to the Ministry of Environment and Tourism (MET). Drafting a constitution, definition of membership and boundaries, as well as the election of a representative committee, are the first steps that community members must negotiate to qualify for registration as a conservancy. Once the ministry is satisfied that all requirements have been fulfilled, conservancy status is granted. The conservancy is then a legal entity, free to enter into commercial agreements with the private sector.

The Torra Conservancy

The Torra Conservancy was one of the first communities to mobilise and register themselves toward the end of 1998. Straddling the basalt-strewn Grootberg Mountains, livestock husbandry and migrant labour dominate the livelihoods of its sparsely distributed residents. The modest stone office at Bergsig near Khorixas is the nerve centre of this remarkably successful enterprise that boasts around 400 members. A stream of visiting journalists, film crews and development workers attest to the model status Torra has achieved. With an area of 8 000 square kilometres, Torra is home to significant numbers of wildlife, including elephant, giraffe and rhino. A luxury, tented safari camp, along with lucrative hunting safaris

operated from within conservancy boundaries, has injected significant revenue into conservancy coffers. Torra has been, from the outset, the benchmark for the model in the region.

Other communities in the region have registered or are in the process of completing the often-laborious task of fulfilling the requirements to register. Some neighbouring communities have found the setting of conservancy boundaries a thorny issue. Communal, open-access grazing has also created tension, highlighting the need for revision of existing land tenure legislation to complement the conservancy concept. Current conservancy legislation only applies to wildlife resources. In some areas political and ethnic rivalries, as well as village politics, have taken centre stage, nullifying the very concept of 'community'. Stakes are high with potentially lucrative tourism and hunting concessions up for renegotiation.

The Torra Conservancy, one of the first communities to mobilise and register in 1998.

BONIFATIUS AWARAB
Torra Conservancy, Bergsig

Mention the name Boni Awarab at practically any locale in north-western Namibia and you will be met with smiles of recognition. The inaugural chair of the Torra Conservancy is well liked. His dark, rather imposing façade and bass voice have the ability to intimidate. Fortunately, a mischievous ivory grin and genial personality soon temper this image.

Boni grew up in the shadow of the Brandberg massif at Sorros Sorros on the Ugab River, raised, as is often the custom, by his grandparents. His Roman Catholic mission education is still evident in his capable command of several languages, as well as his teetotal habits. Like other families in the region, semi-nomadic pastoralism combined with periods working on Namibia's mines have defined the working history of many of the Awarab menfolk. Boni spent his early career driving heavy-duty trucks at the now defunct tin mine at Uis. The family and their livestock make regular local migrations from their Rooivlak home at the foot of the Grootberg Mountains in search of water and grazing. Boni's day job is as senior guide at the nearby Etendeka Mountain Camp. With an engaging manner, he educates the largely foreign audience that visits here about the natural heritage of the area.

ON GETTING THE TORRA CONSERVANCY OFF THE GROUND . . .

We encountered a lot of suspicion from the community when we put the concept to them. Some thought it was a scheme to enrich committee members. It took a long time, many meetings, to get them to trust us and understand the concept. We still have some minor problems such as a boundary dispute to the south, but overall things are moving ahead.

ON IRDNC'S INVOLVEMENT . . .

IRDNC has provided technical and logistical support from the start, as well as contributing half of our running costs. This will be phased out over time as we earn more revenue and become self-sufficient.

ON ADMINISTRATION AND REVENUE . . .

We're responsible for the salaries of six game guards, who are chosen by the community. They are responsible for monitoring wildlife numbers as well as accompanying tourists, visitors and hunters on the conservancy. We have an agreement with Wilderness Safaris, Namibia, who run Damaraland Camp as a concession on conservancy land. They pay annual rent as well as a bed-night levy. We've also had a hunting outfitter who brought in clients to hunt various animals. We've opened a bank account where all income is deposited. We also have some income invested in a savings scheme. This revenue is available for use by the conservancy. We're considering a number of projects for funding. These include helping to set up small, income-generating businesses, funding infrastructural development at the school and a possible household stipend. Conservancy members also suffer stock and crop losses to large mammals. Compensation may be offered, as government is not always able to meet these costs. All these proposals are discussed with members to see how they want the money spent.

ON HUNTING . . .

Hunting can be very lucrative: an elephant goes for somewhere around N$60 000. (US$10 000) The hunting outfitter will hopefully return, as he was happy with how things went last year.

ON THE FUTURE . . .

We have an agreement with Wilderness Safaris to take over Damaraland Camp in 2007. This means we need to have staff trained to fulfil these roles. Many school-leavers are without jobs and spend most of the time doing very little at home, so we'd like to train our younger conservancy members in tourism management as well as in other skills.

Boni in his 'day' job as a guide at Etendeka Mountain Camp.

CAMPFIRE: the Zimbabwe model

However, not all areas have the same potential for success. In Zimbabwe, CAMPFIRE critics assert that it is bureaucratic, donor dependent and overly reliant on sport hunting for revenue generation at the district level. Districts with limited wildlife resources, particularly elephant, have posted modest returns. Moves to diversify sources of income in the Zimbabwean model include eco-tourism ventures, as well as a possible change in legislation giving communities rights over mineral resources. Critics of the local conservancy programme are uneasy with the new status quo that has empowered local people. They maintain that communities are not equipped for the complex task of natural resource management, and that existing government structures are the appropriate agents to administer this duty. Biosphere reserves and contractual national parks, where the state retains some measure of authority, are the suggested alternatives.

Contractual national parks

Opponents argue that contractual national parks (CNP) are undesirable because ultimate control continues to rest with government agencies, whilst local people remain marginalised. The North-West was, in fact, proposed as a CNP in 1988–1989, and as such would have shared benefits with the local communities, but only on the terms dictated by the relevant government ministry. Critics venture that a top-down conservation policy succeeds only with a powerful and well-resourced administration that can implement rules. However, they contend that the last decade has seen the erosion of the ministry's capacity and assert that this trend is likely to continue.

Kuva Rutari, young Himba and community game guard.

The draft tourism master-plan for the region identifies an urgent and definite need to regulate tourism. How does one achieve this in an area that isn't a national park or game reserve? IRDNC believes that conservancies are the answer. The organisation evolved out of the auxiliary game guard scheme of the early eighties, the aim of which was to link the conservation and sustainable use of wildlife and other natural resources to the social and economic development of rural communities. Set up with the support and initiative of local traditional leaders, the scheme was essentially the embryo of the conservancies and illustrated that local people were capable of taking on responsibility.

Torra Conservancy game guards John Awarab and Markus Roman record wildlife observations using GPS-generated maps. The game guards are the eyes and ears of the conservancy, and patrol the area relentlessly. All the data that is collected is collated and added to the conservancy database.

Owen-Smith and Jacobsohn: an alternative vision

Harnessing substantial international donor funding, IRDNC have actively championed the contemporary cause of the conservancy initiative. The founders and co-directors of IRDNC, Garth Owen-Smith and Dr Margaret Jacobsohn, lead an itinerant life. The bureaucracy involved in managing this dynamic organisation, coupled with visits to field projects around the country, mean they often spend only a few days a month at their nominal home – the aptly named Wêreldsend. From this modest base, buildings crouched under spartan Damaraland shade, they direct the activities of an industrious team. Owen-Smith has the air of a distinguished statesman about him, an image tempered by the faded blue denim trousers he invariably wears. Jacobsohn is lucid, articulate and direct in a manner that can be perturbing. With their divergent approaches, they complement each other professionally – Owen-Smith, the patient and cautious diplomat, Jacobsohn ardently reflecting her progressive roots.

Their combined efforts are widely attributed with halting the decimation of the Kunene region's wildlife. A clutch of international environmental awards, which include the prestigious Goldman Environmental Prize for Africa, have found a home on the Wêreldsend mantelpiece. Owen-Smith and Jacobsohn are well known for espousing a philosophy that empowers rural communities and preserves the diverse wildlife of the region. They highlight the need for an alternative 'vision' for rural education, both in Namibia and in Africa as a whole, to counter the deficiencies of Western education and Eurocentric values that have been a major hindrance to the environment.

IRDNC actively participated in the five-year period of consultations and socio-ecological surveys that preceded the gazetting of the new conservancy legislation in 1996, resulting in the new policy on

Torra Conservancy game guard Markus Roman makes a point after observing a rhino cow with her two calves. Most rhino are identified by the shape and size of their horns, as well as by the territory they inhabit.

wildlife management, utilisation and tourism in communal areas. Since then, the organisation's primary role has been to develop the capacity of the communal area conservancies, enabling them to manage their objectives and to generate income. It also provides technical support, training and interim financial and logistical support. There are currently nine registered conservancies countrywide and another fifteen in the pipeline, with more than 100 community game guards in the Kunene and Caprivi regions alone. This amounts to two million hectares currently under conservancy status, with the potential for a total of six million, a significant area with tremendous developmental potential.

Owen-Smith and Jacobsohn maintain that, with the breakdown of traditional structures throughout Africa, a conservancy offers a grass-roots structure that can be adapted to local circumstance – a social organisation that facilitates development. Dismissing accusations of autocracy in the implementation of the conservancy initiative, Jacobsohn disputes allegations that the institution of conservancies is imposed and insists that IRDNC's role is to build up the communities' capacity – not to dictate what they should do. The two directors believe that there are misconceptions amongst the local business elite who do not have a good understanding of the basic ethos of conservancies – challengers who believe that there is no room within the conservancy for private business. Owen-Smith and Jacobsohn are adamant, however, that the opposite is, in fact, the case: local entrepreneurs simply have to draw up a contract with the conservancy in the same way that any other investor would.

Necessary ingredients for success

IRDNC's vision, the commercial success of Namibia's conservancies, is partially dependent on external determinants. Tourism and sport hunting both rely on private sector investment and expertise in marketing and servicing western markets. Moreover, regional political stability will inevitably dictate if fickle tourists continue to arrive on these shores. For a region with spartan wildlife populations, hunting will never be the financial panacea it has been for some Zimbabwean communities. Rural stakeholders are also in danger of having unrealistic expectations of a model that is designed to complement existing land-use practices – not replace them.

In its favour, the Namibian initiative has not assumed, but stressed, the management of wildlife resources, with potential benefits following thereafter. Conservancies are, therefore, in a probationary period. Time will test their efficacy and demonstrate if they are capable of sustaining themselves financially – whilst delivering equitable returns for members. The necessary ingredients are certainly available to enable diversification of the current economic base. The traditional obstacles of power and control over resources are clearly no longer a factor – neglected rural communities have eventually been accorded long overdue respect. Conservancies, with their adaptive character and autonomy from government, would appear to have solid foundations in enabling them to achieve their goals.

Joel Ganaseb is a community game guard of many years' standing, having been recruited in the mid-1980s. His son, Mannetjie, has followed him into a career in conservation.

EPILOGUE

'It is our duty to proceed from what is near to what is distant, from what is known to that which is less known, to gather the traditions from those who have reported them, to correct them as much as possible and to leave the rest as it is, in order to make our work help anyone who seeks truth and loves wisdom.'

Abu'l-Rayhan Muhamad al-Biruni, AD 973-1050

'Always lightly tread.'

E Cronje Wilmot

LOCAL CONTACTS

ORGANISATIONS

Desert Research Foundation of Namibia (DRFN)
PO Box 20232
Windhoek
Tel: 061 229855
Fax: 061 230172

Integrated Rural Development and Nature Conservation (IRDNC)
PO Box 9681
Kenya House
2nd Floor
Windhoek
Tel: 061 228506/9
Fax: 061 228530
E-mail: irdnc@iafrica.com.na

Namibia Community Based Tourism Association (NACOBTA)
PO Box 86099
18 Liliencron St
Windhoek
Tel: 061 250558
Fax: 061 22647
E-mail: nacobta@iafrica.com.na

Namibia Scientific Society
PO Box 67
J Meinart St
Windhoek
Tel: 061 225372
Fax: 061 226846
E-mail: nwg@iafrica.com.na

Namibian Nature Foundation (NNF)
PO Box 245
Windhoek
Tel: 061 248245
Fax: 061 248344
E-mail: ddirector@nnf.org.na

Save the Rhino Trust (SRT)
PO Box 224
Swakopmund
Tel: 064 403829
E-mail: srt@rhino-trust.org.na

Worldwide Fund for Nature (WWF)
PO Box 9681
68/A Robert Mugabe Avenue
Windhoek
Tel: 061 239945
Fax: 061 239799

TOUR OPERATORS

Bicornis Safaris
PO Box 224
Swakopmund
Tel: 064 403829
E-mail: srt@rhino-trust.org.na

Etendeka Mountain Camp
PO Box 24
Kamanjab
Tel/Fax: 061 226979
E-mail: logufa@mweb.com.na

Kaoko Himba Safaris
PO Box 11580
Windhoek
Tel/Fax: 061 222378
E-mail: kaokohimba@natron.net

Mobile Safaris (D Gilchrist)
PO Box 22
Kamanjab
Tel/Fax: 067 330035

Wilderness Safaris
PO Box 6850
8 Bismarck St
Windhoek
Tel: 061 225178
Fax: 061 239455

Wildheart Journeys
PO Box 80401
Windhoek
Tel: 061 259725
Fax: 061 233890
E-mail:
wildheartjourneys@iafrica.com.na

SOURCES

Bollig, M. (1998). In Hayes, P (ed) *et al.*
*Namibia under South African Rule: Mobility
and Containment 1915–1946.* James
Currey/Out of Africa/Ohio University Press,
Athens/London/Windhoek.

Carruthers, J. (1995). *The Life and Work of
Thomas Baines.* Fernwood Press, Cape Town,
South Africa.

Centre Technique Forestier Tropical, trans.
*Wood, PJ. (1989). Faidherbia Albida – A
Monograph.* CTFT, France.

Clement, AJ. (1975). James Chapman:
Pioneer Photographer. *SWA Yearbook*,
Windhoek, Namibia.

Craven, P and Marais, C. (1992).
Damaraland Flora. Gamsberg Macmillan,
Windhoek, Namibia.

Curtis, B. (2000). *Commiphora of Namibia.*
(Part1–3) Namibia Tree Atlas Project, Windhoek.

Du Pisani, E. (1978). *Dama Settlement and
Subsistence Along the Ugab Valley, Namibia.*
Research Papers of the National Museum,
Bloemfontein.

Estes, RD. (1995). *The Behaviour Guide to
African Mammals.* Russell Friedman Books,
Halfway House, South Africa.

Grunert, N. (2000). *Namibia – Fascination
of Geology, A Travel Handbook.*
Klaus Hess Publishers, Windhoek/
Gottingen.

Hall-Martin, A, Walker, C and Bothma, J du
P. (1988). *Kaokoveld – The Last Wilderness.*
Southern Books, Bergvlei, Johannesburg,
South Africa.

Hodgson, FDI and Botha, BJV (1978).
The Damara Supergroup in the Area around
the Doros Complex, South West Africa.
Annals of the Geological Survey, vol. II:
pp.139-145. Windhoek.

Immelman, D. (1977). Dorsland trek. *SWA
Yearbook*, Windhoek, Namibia.

Jacobsohn, M. (1995) *Negotiating Meaning
and Change in Space and Material Culture –
An ethno-archaeological study among semi-
nomadic Himba and Herero herders in north-
western Namibia.* University of Cape Town.

Jacobsohn, M, Pickford, P and Pickford, B.
(1990). *Himba – Nomads of Namibia.* Struik
Publishers, Cape Town, South Africa.

Jacobson, NHG. (1988). Euphorbias of the
Skeleton Coast National Park: Namibia and
Adjacent Areas. *The Euphorbia Journal*, vol. V,
Strawberry Press, California, USA.

Jacobson, PJ, Jacobson, KM and Seely MK.
(1995). *Ephemeral Rivers and Their
Catchments – Sustaining People and
Development in Western Namibia.* Desert
Research Foundation of Namibia, Windhoek,
Namibia.

Jarvis, A and Robertson, T. (1999). Namibia's
Inland Endemics. *Africa – Birds and Birding,*
April/May. Black Eagle Publishing, Cape
Town, South Africa.

Joubert, E. (1971). The Past and Present
Distribution and Status of the Black
Rhinoceros *(Diceros bicornis Linn.* 1758) in
South West Africa. *Madoqua,* vol 1 (4): pp.
33-43.

Joubert, E. (1996). *On the Clover Trail – The
Plight of the World's Rhinos.* Gamsberg
Macmillan, Windhoek, Namibia.

Jurgens, N, Burke, A, Seely, MK and
Jacobson, KM. (1997). *Vegetation of Southern
Africa* (ed. RM Cowling). Cambridge
University Press,

Cambridge,U.K.

Kingdon, J. (1989). *Island Africa – The
Evolution of Africa's Rare Animals and Plants.*
Princeton University Press, Princeton, New
Jersey.

Legal Assistance Centre. (1998). *The Epupa
Debate.* Legal Assistance Centre, Windhoek,
Namibia.

Legget, K, Fennessy, J, Schneider, S. (2000).
*A Preliminary Study of the Elephants of the
Hoanib River Catchment, Northwest Namibia.*
Desert Research Foundation of Namibia.
Windhoek.

Lewis-Williams, D, Dowson, T. (1989).
*Images of Power – Understanding Bushman
Rock Art.* Southern Books, Halfway House,
South Africa.

Loutit, BD, Reuter, HO. (1998). *Mission
Statement.* Save the Rhino Trust,
Swakopmund, Namibia.

Loutit, BD, Louw, GW and Seely, MK.
(1987). First approximation of food preferences and the chemical composition of the
diet of the desert dwelling black rhinoceros,
Diceros bicornis L. Madoqua, vol. 15 (1): pp.
35-54.

Lovegrove, B. (1993). *The Living Deserts of
Southern Africa.* Fernwood Press, Cape Town.

Maclean, GL. (1974). Arid-Zone Adaptations
in Southern African Birds. *Cimbebasia A:* pp.
163-176.

Malan, JS. (1995). *Peoples of Namibia.* Rhino
Publishers, South Africa.

Marsh, BA. (1990). The micro-environment
associated with Welwitschia mirabilis in the

Namib Desert. In: Seely, MK. (ed) *Namib Ecology: 25 years of Namib research.* Transvaal Museum Monograph No.7, Transvaal Museum, Pretoria.

Miescher, G. Henrichsen, D (eds) (2000). *New Notes on Kaoko – The Northern Kunene Region (Namibia) in Texts and Photographs.* Basler Afrika Bibliographen, Switzerland.

Moll, E and Witt, B. (1996). Plants and Sex. *African Wildlife*, vol. 50 (2)..

Namibia Oral Tradition Project (1996). *The Moon People and Other Namibian Stories.* New Namibian Books, Windhoek, Namibia.

Newman, K. (1997). *Birds of Southern Africa.* Southern Books, Halfway House, South Africa.

Noli, D and Avery, G. (1987). Stone circles in the Cape Fria Area, Northern Namibia. *The South African Archaeological Bulletin*, vol. XLII (145).

Owen-Smith, GL. (1986). The Kaokoveld, South West Africa/Namibia's Threatened Wilderness. *African Wildlife*, vol. 40 (3). Johannesburg.

Schoeman, A. (1996). *Skeleton Coast.* Southern Books, Halfway House, South Africa.

Skinner, JD and Smithers RHN. (1990). The Mammals of Southern Africa. University of Pretoria, South Africa.

Van Warmelo, NJ. (1962). Notes on the Kaokoveld (South West Africa) and its People. Department of Bantu Administration, *Ethnological Publications* No. 26, The Government Printer, Pretoria, South Africa.

Viljoen, PJ. (1982). The Distribution and Population Status of the Larger Mammals in the Kaokoland, South West Africa/ Namibia. *Cimbebasia A* (7): pp. 5-33.

Viljoen, PJ. (1988). *The Ecology of the Desert-Dwelling Elephants* Loxodonta Africana *(Blumenbach, 1797) of Western Damaraland and Kaokoland.* PhD. Thesis, University of Pretoria, Pretoria, South Africa.

Vogel, JC and Rust, U. (1987). Environmental changes in the Kaokoland Namib Desert during the present millennium. *Madoqua*, vol. 15 (1): pp. 5-16.

Von Maydell, HJ. (1986). *Trees and Shrubs of the Sahel – Their Characteristics and Uses.* GTZ, Germany.

Von Wyk, WL. (1971). The Geological History of South West Africa. *SWA Yearbook*, Windhoek, Namibia.

Walker, C. (1978). Kaokoveld: Who is doing the killing now? *African Wildlife*, vol. 32 (6).

White, A, Dyer, A and Sloane, BL. (1941). *The Succulent Euphorbiaceae (Southern Africa).* Abbey Garden Press, Pasadena, California, U.S.A.

INDEX